TUTORING IN SPORT

...a working guide

Rick Cross
Paul Robbins
Lynn Hogarth

TUTORING IN SPORT

Rick Cross
Paul Robbins
Lynn Hogarth

Front cover illustration – Derek Matthews

First published in Great Britain in 1999

by Cross, Robbins & Hogarth

33 Ermine Street, Thundridge, Ware Herts SG12 0SY

ISBN 0 9537211 0 8

Printed and bound by Hertford Offset Limited, Hertford

We would particularly like to thank Roy Collins for acting as our "Tutor in the Street" when we were creating draft manuscripts of the book. His comments were invaluable in helping us to remain focused. We also acknowledge our debt to the hundreds of candidates at a variety of levels, some of whom are now tutors themselves, who have suffered at our tutoring hands over the years. Our work with them has taught us more about tutoring than they could possibly ever realise.

Contents

Contents

Contents

This publication focuses on the many issues that hit both experienced and inexperienced tutors in the running of courses, elaborates on the possible implications and suggests possible answers to the many practical issues which arise in the process. It also considers the practicalities of developing and maintaining standards, the responsibilities of assessing as accurately as possible in relation to those standards, and possible methods by which tutors can approach their very important and influential contribution to the maintenance of standards in their sport.

One of the reasons why people take up teaching/coaching is a feeling that they can contribute to the sport/discipline by giving their time and expertise to encourage others in their personal development. Often, of course, and depending on the discipline, they will also admit to a potential increase in income as being another factor! What is often overlooked is the influence a tutor can have on the particular discipline(s) in which they have an interest. The long-term influence of good tutoring at all levels, and all disciplines, is considerable when it is reflected through the candidate teachers/coaches who pass through their hands, and then on to the participants with whom they subsequently work.

The role, professional image, and impact of a tutor carry enormous responsibilities. Part of that impact should also be reflected in firing the enthusiasm of teachers/coaches to pursue further knowledge and techniques through opportunities in Continuing Professional Development (CPD).

I can't teach you anything, I can only help you learn
- Galileo, 1564-1642

Part 1

Tutoring – The Overview

1.0   The Role

The role of a tutor can be described as:

"Facilitating candidate learning by creating an environment which helps that individual increase their level of competence in pre-determined, specific areas."

The tutor needs to create situations that will allow candidates to experience the use of skills and the application of knowledge so that they gain understanding and learn by 'doing' rather than simply gathering data. In order to do this tutors should consider how:

- **to create a learning environment** by using methods such as briefings, lessons, lectures, small/large group work and by giving feedback to individual candidates and groups in a variety of situations. This may be in the classroom or in an external teaching/coaching environment. The production of tutor notes, design of exercises and case studies for individuals and groups is an important aspect of this element
- **to demonstrate** the required skills so that candidates can "record" the image and use it as a reference model against which to assess their own performance. This may be a swimming stroke, a javelin throw, how to run a teaching/coaching session, or even how to handle an irate parent
- **to facilitate**, including helping individuals and groups of candidates in their personal development when they are placed in the learning situation. This is a vital skill for an interactive tutor
- **to act as a leader and manager** of the candidates, participants and the resources used within the learning situation
- **to use a variety of techniques and methods** within the learning environment. (See Part 1, paragraph 1.5, *Creating a Learning Environment* and paragraph 1.6, *Dealing with Questions*).

1.2   The Person

Perhaps a good way to decide on the qualities and competencies required of the person to do this job would be to place an imaginary advertisement in a magazine. How would it be worded?

"Wanted, excellent tutor able to provide effective training for teachers/coaches. The successful individual must be able to create an environment conducive to

learning for candidates embarking on National Governing Body teaching/coaching courses. Acting as a role model they will be skilled in leadership, management, and facilitation and must have the necessary technical background and qualifications to deliver course material using a variety of interactive techniques".

Person Specification

The person specification defined in the above advertisement will be based on qualities, knowledge and skills which will be reflected in the individual's behaviour and attitude.

- **Qualities**

Enthusiasm	Integrity
Patience	Positive outlook
Honesty	Adaptability
Fairness	And so on…

- **Technical Knowledge**

  Sports specific (usually through NGB qualifying courses or experience)
  Tutoring methods
  Leadership
  Management
  Facilitation
  Tools/Techniques

- **Skills**

  Sports specific application of knowledge, e.g., demonstration of a skill
  Creating a learning environment, e.g., running a lesson or group session
  Demonstrations, e.g., how to deal with a dissatisfied parent Facilitation, e.g., intervening, questioning, counselling, and reviewing Leadership, e.g., communication, motivation, and delegation
  Management, e.g., planning, organising, and controlling
  Coaching, e.g., assessment and feedback on performance
  Problem solving, e.g., decision-making and managing conflict.

1.3   The Job

Job Specification
In writing a job specification the responsibilities would include:

- planning and organising the course to meet the requirements of the NGB syllabus

- planning and preparing for both theory and practical sessions, liaising with the course organiser as appropriate, together with any personal presentation notes in order to meet candidates' needs and maximise their learning

- designing tasks for individuals and groups to allow candidates to gain active experiences on competencies required. These will be derived from the course syllabus

- creating a learning environment which would include briefings, lectures, lessons, and small/large groups in a classroom or practical situation

- using a variety of techniques to support the learning process and make best use of time available

- demonstrating sport specific skills, methods of teaching/coaching individuals and teams of participants, managing difficult situations and positioning in relation to participants when communicating

- facilitating individuals and groups during activities/tasks set by the tutor in order to maximise candidate learning. (Appropriate application of facilitation skills is essential to effective tutoring and requires an understanding of group dynamics)

- providing effective leadership for the course candidates, communicating clearly, motivating to maximise performance and delegating where possible

- problem solving and decision-making to ensure the smooth running of the course is essential

- managing the course through effective planning, organising, and control of resources and candidates to ensure the best use of time and space

- observing candidate performance, assessment and timely feedback to candidates to ensure outcomes and course objectives are met

- handling of conflicts that might arise through all phases of the process.

Task 1 - How do I measure up?

Before doing the exercise it might be useful to have a brief look at the rest of the book as a reminder of all the competencies needed to perform this challenging role.

Personal development planner

1. Identify areas for personal development by deciding on your own current perceived level of competence and try to score yourself on a scale of 1 to 5 (5 is 'very competent' and 1 is 'not competent').

2. Using the same scale, indicate the relative importance you would give to each competence.

3. By selecting low scores on competence against high scores on importance the completed form will help you design an action plan for personal improvement or further research.

	Current Competence	Importance	Section/ Page ref
Designing & organising a course	❏	❏	......
Detailed planning for a course	❏	❏	......
Delivering a briefing/lecture	❏	❏	......
Conducting a lesson	❏	❏	......
Running a group discussion	❏	❏	......
Running a group session	❏	❏	......
Running a role play session	❏	❏	......
Use of tutoring tools & techniques	❏	❏	......
Conducting a demonstration session	❏	❏	......
Demonstrating a sport related skill	❏	❏	......
Facilitating groups and individuals	❏	❏	......
Assessing candidates	❏	❏	......
Giving feedback (written and oral)	❏	❏	......
Leading the team	❏	❏	......
Handling conflict	❏	❏	......

Now try to formulate an action plan to improve your tutoring skills using the sections of this book as your guide.

1.4   How People Learn

Learning can be defined as:

"The acquisition of new skills, knowledge or attitudes which can be demonstrated by a change in an individual's behaviour."

Learning is a complex process which involves taking input from the external world, from experiences and the use of our senses, analysing this input using our thought processes, then planning and committing ourselves to going on to new experiences. There are several stages involved in this process which includes the external aspects of 'doing' and 'sensing', together with the internal elements of 'thinking' and 'planning'. Tutors should recognise that different individuals will take varying degrees of learning from each of these stages. Although all stages are essential to the learning process few individuals will develop in all four areas equally well. We all tend to learn in different ways and, therefore, tutors need to take account of this at the individual level if they are going to help candidates in their personal development.

It is important that the focus is on increasing competence, rather than simply transferring knowledge. Competence, which is a combination of knowledge, skills and attitude reflected in changes of behaviour, includes the 'doing' part and is extremely important. Listening to how to perform a simple task does not have the same level of difficulty as doing it. Juggling looks so easy until we try it ourselves. The theory is one thing, but the application is very different when the balls are tossed up.

In summary, a good tutor helps candidates learn in different ways and tries to identify individual 'learning styles'. Some candidates will learn more from the experience of doing whilst others will take their learning from thinking about the experience after the activity. Learning is greatly enhanced when it is conducted in a supportive environment and where positive feedback is given to individuals on their performance.

The tutor, therefore, has the responsibility of ensuring that learning objectives are achieved by:

- identifying how individuals will learn best, e.g., questionnaires, discussions etc
- establishing candidates' needs for the training event (from syllabus and individual feedback)
- selecting interactive methods to meet course objectives/outcomes and candidates' needs
- creating a supportive environment to maximise learning.

1.5   Creating a Learning Environment

Methods

For any given situation some methods of facilitating learning are more effective than others, and much depends on time constraints and the candidates' current level of competence. The tutor needs to select the method which is appropriate so that learning is maximised but, at the same time, allowing for the individuals' own learning styles.

Figure 1 below suggests the degree to which a method is tutor or candidate "centred" in terms of who provides most of the input/interaction. It is important to recognise that candidates' understanding increases with their level of participation but the time allocations for each session will need to rise accordingly.

Figure 1 – Learning methods

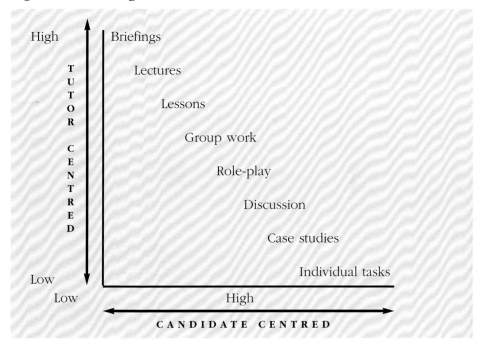

Definition of Learning Methods

- **Briefings** - These are most suitable for general information known only to, and delivered by, the tutor. Some form of documented handout sometimes supports them. Answers to questions from candidates will be limited and confined to clarification of the factual information within the brief, e.g., information delivered to candidates about the course timetable.
(Tutor input is 'high' and candidate interaction is 'low').

- **Lecture** - Delivery of technical information by the tutor to the candidates in order to meet the course syllabus requirements, at times supported by documented handouts or book references – beware, handouts can be documents which pass from the hand of the tutor to the hand of the candidate without passing through the minds of either! Questions will be generally limited to clarification of factual information only, with minimal input from the candidates, e.g., a presentation on the functions of the heart. Because of their backgrounds some candidates, e.g., a sports scientist, may already be familiar with the subject matter, but the tutor will still need to

ensure that all candidates understand the material.
(Tutor input is 'high' and candidate interaction is 'low').

- **Lesson** - Delivery of technical, sport specific information by the tutor but, also, involving the candidates to some degree by giving them the opportunity to add their own experiences and/or knowledge to the subject in order to assist group learning, e.g., a classroom exercise to brainstorm the qualities of a good teacher/coach. Exercises with candidates working in pairs or threes following some technical input from the tutor are further examples of this method, e.g., writing a session plan. The latter is important when candidates need to apply knowledge and practice new skills.
(Tutor input is 'medium' and candidate interaction is 'medium').

- **Discussion** - On a subject related to the course syllabus whereby all candidates are given the opportunity to speak. Input from the tutor is limited to a facilitation or chairmanship role (This can be delegated with mature candidates). Subjects where one individual's opinion is as valid as any other, and where the collective experiences will assist learning, are best dealt with using this method, e.g., a discussion on "How to Teach/coach Children in a Range of Environments".
(Tutor input is 'low' and candidate interaction is 'high').

- **Group Work** - This varies from small groups of candidates, usually pairs or teams of three working for short periods during a lesson, to larger groups of between four to six working in groups/syndicates, performing more complex tasks and skill practices set by the tutor. Here the tutor's contribution comprises some technical input at the beginning, followed by a longer period of time spent by the group members on the task set. The tutor's technical input at the beginning of the session is essential, otherwise it could be seen as abdicating responsibility and not providing sufficient training for the task at hand. If learning is to be maximised facilitation by the tutor during this type of activity is a critical skill.
(Tutor input is 'low' and candidate interaction is 'high').

- **Role-Play** - This is effective for giving candidates an opportunity to experience what it feels like interacting with others in a variety of situations, e.g., asking one participant to play the part of an irate parent whilst another plays the teacher/coach. The format can vary from partner work to larger groups.
(Tutor input is 'low' and candidate interaction is 'high').

- **Case Study** - This is a documented scenario which details a specific situation which a teacher/coach might meet. Individuals who are asked to solve a problem or make a recommendation based on the data can either work individually or in groups.

  (Tutor input is 'low' and candidate interaction is 'high').

- **Individual Tasks** - These could be either homework or practical, course based, activities where the individuals are expected to work on their own. This gives the tutor an opportunity of facilitating learning at the individual level whilst making assessments of candidate progress, e.g., homework set by the tutor to test knowledge or skill or give an incentive for study/research. (See also Part 4, Paragraph 4.6, *The Testing of Understanding*).

  (Tutor input is dependent on the candidate and interaction is 'very high').

The degree of candidate participation in these methods will determine the levels of learning and understanding. There will be a need, therefore, to carefully control time if the course objectives and candidate participation are to be met. It is difficult to suggest proportions of one method versus another because the aims/objectives of the session will determine the approach. Clearly, the greater the candidate participation, the greater the time required.

Tools and Techniques

The efficiency of running a course and, perhaps, the saving of time, will be improved by the application of a variety of tools and techniques in any of the previous situations.

Two of the more common tools and techniques are detailed below:

- **Brainstorming** - This technique can be used by individuals or groups on any subject specified. The aim is to generate as much output as possible in the shortest time and record the information on flip charts or wall boards. This data is then structured for further analysis.

  The process/rules are as follows:
  - Encourage all ideas/issues and allow individuals to 'freewheel'.
  - Try for quantity of ideas/issues rather than quality and include humour!
  - All ideas or issues must be written on a flip chart or wallboard.
  - Use the individual's own words when recording. This shows respect.
  - There must be no criticism or discussion as this wastes time.
  - Incubate for a short time and repeat the exercise.
  - Structure the ideas/issues for discussion and analysis.

- **Consensus Reaching** - Candidates working in small groups are normally required to present findings to the whole group on conclusion of an exercise or task. Sometimes it is difficult for them to agree on the group view and valuable time can be lost in arguments. Consensus reaching offers a structured approach to 'agreeing' the collective view.

  The process/rules are as follows:
  - List the differing views, ideas, suggestions or alternatives.
  - Display them in a prominent position.
  - Check understanding especially on those with greatest disagreement.
  - Vote on the items.
  - Reach a consensus view.

  Not everyone will necessarily be happy with the choice, but at least everyone will have had an input and a chance to put forward a personal view. This then becomes an agreed majority.

1.6   Dealing with Questions

During the course or event candidates will raise many questions as they wrestle to understand new concepts and apply new learning. Most of these questions will arise during formal lectures/lessons or demonstrations but, even when they are outside these occasions, the method of handling them will be the same.

How should a tutor handle questions?
No matter the nature of the question, or the manner in which it has been put, it is important that the same care and attention be given to answering as was devoted to the preparation of any relevant course material.

The rules associated with handling questions are:
- maintain the candidates' self esteem
- avoid being flippant, even if annoyed
- answer concisely
- reply with tact and patience
- be polite and sincere
- be honest
- ensure that the facts are technically accurate.

Handling questions in a formal situation

Question time in a formal setting, such as a lecture/lesson, can prove to be an ordeal, even though the tutor may be very knowledgeable and has planned and prepared the session. However, this kind of feedback often indicates whether or not the objectives for the session have been achieved.

Potential Problems
- **Candidates' response is a complete silence**

   Candidates tend to ask genuine questions for one of two reasons:
   - They have failed to understand/remember part of the delivery and wish to clarify the information.
   - They have understood what has been said but are seeking additional information.

   Failure to receive questions may be because:
   - the subject was clearly explained, but the candidates are still assimilating what has been said
   - the presentation has not generated any interest in the subject (Failure to stimulate interest in the subject may require a rethink about the session)
   - the candidates have not been able to relate to the subject
   - the presentation was poor and confused them too much
   - nobody wants to be first to put a question
   - the candidates feel overawed by the status of the tutor
   - the candidates are tired after a long session (If this is the case, perhaps the structure of the session needs reviewing).

If the candidates genuinely have no questions then they should be thanked for their attention and the proceedings closed. It is also useful if tutors remind the candidates of their availability in case any points of difficulty arise later. On those occasions, when the candidates are merely being coy, the tutor could ask a general question or fill in with... *"A question I often ask is..."*, which might encourage them to talk. Candidates feel better about asking questions if they totally trust the tutor's responses. If they feel that they are going to made to feel foolish in public they are unlikely to speak up. For every one person who asks a question there are probably at least three others who also wanted to raise the issue, but lacked the courage to do so. If it is clear that nobody wishes to ask a question do not prolong things by desperately fishing for one!

- **Has it been heard and understood?**
  When a question has been received the tutor should ensure that everyone has both heard and understood it so:
  - repeat it
  - rephrase it, if appropriate, and put it back to the questioner to confirm the correct understanding
  - if the meaning of the question is unclear, admit it and ask for it to be put again using different phraseology.

- **Red herrings**
  Sometimes questions are raised which only have a vague connection with the subject and about which the tutor knows little. Conversely, it may be some aspect of the subject about which the tutor is particularly knowledgeable, although still outside the scope of the session. For the sake of other members of the group, who may be waiting to put more pertinent questions, politely and firmly explain why it cannot be covered, but that it might be possible to find discussion time later. If the question is beyond the tutor's knowledge and experience then the best policy is to admit it, but try to suggest someone else who could provide the answer.

- **The tutor does not know the answer**
  It is tempting to side step the question in an attempt to save face but candidates quickly recognise when the tutor really does not have the answer. Be honest, do not bluff, but offer to find out. Try to anticipate what questions are likely to be asked so that provision is made for them at the preparation stage of the session.

- **The display question**
  Some questioners try to 'upstage' the tutor simply as a means of demonstrating their own knowledge. However, since these individuals might also provide some additional information, they should receive careful attention. A similar type of question is designed to probe the tutor's knowledge and experience. Remember the golden rule, do not attempt to bluff!

- **The persistent/hostile questioner**
  Occasionally, individuals in a group:
  - will ask one question after another
  - will continually raise the same issue
  - will seemingly be opposed to either the tutor or the subject being presented.

  This may be because:
  - they are very keen and interested and want to know much more
  - their comments are based on preconceived ideas which have not been altered by the presentation
  - the presentation has included issues about which they have particularly strong views
  - the explanations or line of approach taken does not convince them
  - they are generally aggressive by nature
  - they feel a potential/implied loss of their status or control, e.g., *"I think that coaches rather than teachers should decide on the criteria for awards"*. This is clearly creating unnecessary divisions of interest.

  It is important that these individuals should not be allowed to take over question time or send the other candidates away with a negative attitude towards the subject. Again, if the questioner is enthusiastic and wishes to know much more about the subject, thank him/her for the interest and suggest further discussion will have to take place outside the session. Try to ensure that all candidates who have questions have the opportunity to raise them. If an individual will not accept a point which has already been covered, put forward the related facts concerning the issue and be prepared to agree to differ. Try not to allow a duel of words to develop in public.

  No matter how arrogant or aggressive a questioner may be tutors cannot allow themselves to lose their tempers and risk losing the respect of the remainder of the candidates. Simply state the facts and put forward the relevant positive points. Remember, the individual is entitled to a personal view, which might well remain unmodified, no matter how convincing the arguments.

- **The concealed question**
  Whilst it may only be thinly concealed, e.g., *"Won't this entail more paperwork?"* or, *"Why is the price of the qualification so high?"*, tutors should avoid becoming defensive. Put the question into perspective and give the compensating benefits.

- **Bringing question time to an end**

  Frequently the questions people wish to ask will fill the allotted time and the situation might arise where the session will overrun unless it is brought to a close. Tutors should avoid getting a reputation for overrunning because, not only do they set a bad example to the candidates, it might also mean that they will not be invited to run future programmes. In addition to the tutor keeping a check on the time, the appointment of someone in the group to act as timekeeper might be a useful ploy. Expressions such as "*There is time for just two more questions*", or, "*This will have to be the last one*", will focus on the time constraints. The formal ending of the presentation means that those who wish to leave can do so, whilst anyone who still has a question will have the opportunity to ask it informally.

Remember, the final word is always with the tutor - don't throw it away at the end.

1.7   Handling Conflict

There is always a possibility of conflict arising when human beings form into teams or groups in a formal environment such as a training course. Unless the tutor deals with these situations in a skilful manner there can be serious consequences. To reduce the risk of conflict a heightened awareness of the processes and behaviours operating within the group, especially whilst they are involved in tutor set assignments, is helpful to both the individuals within the group and the tutor. Tutors who are clear about what is going on within their classes can influence that group more easily and reduce possible tension.

Sources of conflict

There are many forces active within a group which can disturb the progress of a task. These forces form an emotional undercurrent and may produce behaviour that will make it difficult for the group to function. Groups often ignore such issues, or wish them away. The effective group member will recognise such matters and then encourage the group to discuss and deal with them openly and, so, remove blocks to progress. When candidates form together on a course and become involved in group activities they will themselves have a number of questions, such as:

What is my role within this group? Where do I fit in? What kind of behaviour is acceptable here? What values do the others in the group live by? What do I want from this group? What's in it for me? Is the group's agenda consistent with mine? What have I to offer the group? Who will control what we do? How much autonomy do the group or I have? How close will we get to each other? And, possibly the most important of all, *How much can we trust each other?*

Unless tutors carefully observe the behaviours and interactions within their groups they are unlikely to note the cues and, thus, be able to reduce tension.

• What should a tutor look for within groups?

The tutor should try to distinguish between process and content to see what is going on. It is not only the tasks that are important; the tutor needs to be aware of both how the tasks are being achieved by the group, and the emotions that are in play. These collectively will determine levels of conflict. The content, i.e., the 'what', deals with the subject matter or task on which the group is working. In most groups this is usually the prime concern with very little attention being paid to the process. The process is the means by which the group achieves a set task, i.e., the 'how'. This can either be structured, and follow a logical sequence involving all candidates, or it can be haphazard, and led by one or a minority of strong individuals. The dangers with the latter are obvious and, therefore, the ability to understand how group decisions are made, and who is controlling the group, becomes a key skill for the tutor. Generally, very little attention is paid to process, even when it is the major cause of conflict within the group. Sensitivity will enable the tutor to diagnose problems early and deal with them more effectively.

• Group behaviour

In order to spot conflicts arising it is important that the tutor carefully monitors, at an individual level, the contribution from all candidates. Look for helpful behaviours such as suggestions and ideas for completing a task; seeking and giving relevant information; clearing confusion and pulling together related information. Less obvious but, nevertheless important, are individuals who attempt to reconcile disagreements and who are friendly, warm and responsive to others. The behaviours a tutor needs to spot, and deal with immediately, are candidates who oppose or resist anyone in the group who represents authority, anyone who dominates the group to get their own way regardless of others, or those candidates who withdraw and fail to make a contribution for long periods.

Conflict handling skills

- By careful observation, and prompt action when necessary, a tutor can stop conflict arising – in most cases! If, however, conflict does emerge the tutor will need to follow a structured process as soon as practicable in order to deal with it.

- The tutor must clearly define the conflict and clarify the details before attempting to take any action. A sympathetic response to people, showing understanding of what they want from the situation and checking this understanding by asking questions, helps to diffuse the situation. By getting to the real feelings, and the reasons for them, the tutor establishes a shared concern, to both solve the problem and agree the harmful effects of the conflict.

  Once this has been done the tutor can ask the group for ideas and, if possible, provide suggestions. Finally, by going through the process of setting outcomes and agreeing actions, the conflict can be resolved.

Further considerations to help minimise conflict:

- At the introductions stage invite any concerns and issues from the candidates and resolve any that relate to the course there and then.
- Note any concerns which cannot be resolved immediately and promise that an attempt will be made to do so as soon as possible. Indicate when this might be.
- Explain that there will be feedback sessions during the course and that candidate views and comments are important for future courses.
- Have a 'Ground Rule' slot and remind everyone that they are not there to reorganise the NGB, that they should respect the views of others and that every attempt will be made to make the course productive. Point out that the course will only work if everyone joins in and supports each other.
- Stress that the course is a supportive environment where all contributions are valued.
- Encourage humour and light banter.
- Make regular checks to ensure that the outcomes are being achieved, and make spot checks by asking questions.
- Be polite, but firm, with anyone who is being deliberately disruptive. Individuals cannot be allowed to spoil the course for everyone else. Deal with the situation early. If necessary take the individual to one side and try to establish the root cause. If the individual needs help offer it, but explain that help is a two way process if the course is to be a success for everyone.
- Try not to look too hard for problems!

Part 2

Designing
and
Organising the Course

2.1 Planning a Course

Introduction

At this stage tutors might find themselves wearing either one or two hats, namely, as tutor, or as a tutor and organiser. Both have advantages and disadvantages.

As both tutor and course organiser

Advantages:
- Total control of course
- Understands requirements

Disadvantages:
- Additional responsibilities
- Can be distracted from tutoring

As tutor only

Advantages:
- Focus solely on candidates
- More time available

Disadvantages:
- Organiser not understanding course requirements and expectations of the tutor
- Organiser not delivering to the expectations of the tutor

Types of courses

Teacher/coach education courses are organised in a variety of ways, usually related to the availability of facilities, candidates, participants and tutors. This means it is difficult to give an ideal example of how to structure a course. There are, however, some structures which are utilised on a reasonably regular basis:

- **Compact course** - This type of course, sometimes called a "concentrated" course, may be either residential or non-residential and involves an intensive programme of tutoring over a number of days, normally during school holiday periods. It permits candidates to focus solely on the task in hand, particularly if they are attending the course on a residential basis.

Not all candidates and tutors relish this type of course. For those intending to tutor a course of this nature it is important that the candidates appreciate the need to arrive fully prepared by completing some work and reading prior to the course commencing. It is also essential that the tutor has impressed upon the candidates the pressure they are likely to encounter.

- **Weekend course** - Some courses are held over a number of weekends. Many candidates find this the ideal solution to attending a course because they may be able to attend without taking time off work. The course is semi-intensive in nature, so it can be completed in a reasonable time frame, but allows the candidate to complete work in the interim period. There is also more time for reflection by the candidates between sessions.

- **Weekly course** - This is probably the most common organisational method. The course spans a number of weeks with a session being held once or twice weekly. This allows time for the candidate to complete work in the non-contact hours during the week, as well as allowing the tutor ample time to prepare for the next session of the course. Another advantage is that candidates get time to try out the skills before the next session. This type of course is also popular with candidates because it fits fairly easily into a busy lifestyle. Depending on the time requirements of the syllabus this type of course can, however, span a very large number of weeks.

- **Combination courses** - It is possible to hold a course which is a combination of any of the methods already mentioned.

2.2   Resource Implications

The resources needed to tutor a course in sport are often far greater than the more traditional academic course. There is usually a requirement for both practical and theory facilities and equipment and, as a result, the selection of course venue needs very careful consideration. This is not always an easy task since, although many sports venues offer superb facilities for the practical aspects of the course, they are often lacking in suitable accommodation for the theory work. Similarly, venues which offer good lecturing accommodation do not always have the sporting facilities required.

The venue for the course must not only meet all the needs of the course syllabus, but it must also be comfortable, accessible and, most importantly, be available at the right times. If the use of a public facility, such as a sports centre, is being considered the time availability constraint can often be one of the greatest stumbling blocks.

● **Professional working relationships**

To ensure that the resources are fully developed it is essential that a wide range of professional working relationships are established. Figure 2 suggests just how wide the network might be.

Figure 2 – Professional relationships

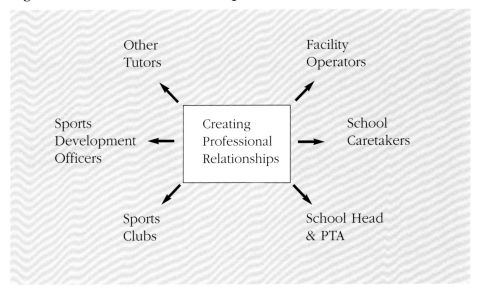

There are many other individuals and organisations contributing to the success of courses, and establishing professional relationships with them is important. No tutor is an island, and it would be a mistake to believe otherwise.

A manager of a public facility would find it useful if the tutor did the following:
● Planned a programme of courses covering, perhaps, the next twelve months.
● Provided detailed information of the facilities and equipment required.
● Discussed the administration of the course.

- Explained any staffing implications.
- Agreed any financial arrangements.
- Confirmed all details in writing.
- Listed the resource implications, including the use of participants for practical work.

The professional relationships developed with a school caretaker may be quite different from the relationship established with the school head. Both are equally important and can both have either a positive or a detrimental effect on courses. The links with other organisations vary from sport to sport but, usually, for inexperienced tutors, the best source of information will be fellow tutors. Many experienced tutors will have organised their practical sessions in different ways and at different venues and will be able to offer sound advice.

Eventually, resources become a matter of customers and suppliers. The success of any course will depend upon the quality of the relationship between customers and suppliers. The tutor should consider their needs carefully and ensure that course content is linked to them.

Customers (who will benefit)
- Course candidates.
- National Governing Bodies.
- Clubs and employers, e.g., Leisure Centres, Local Authorities.
- Participants.

Suppliers (assist delivery)
- Local authorities (facilities).
- Leisure centre staff (facilities and support).
- Clubs (participants, helpers).
- National Governing Bodies.

Having identified as many of these as possible tutors should try to establish a rapport by visiting and talking to them, letting them know what is needed and the value of their potential contribution. The stronger the links and the more positive the relationship, the greater the probability of a successful course outcome.

- ## Resource considerations

Whilst reference has been made to the resource implications in terms of tutors' needs, there must also be consideration for the needs of candidates and participants.

Candidates
- Do they understand the course requirements/commitment?
- Are they able to access the venue easily?
- Does the venue have catering facilities?
- Will the candidate have to purchase additional resources, e.g., textbooks or equipment?

Participants
- Is the venue easy to find?
- Is the venue located a reasonable distance from participants' houses?
- What do the participants need to bring?
- Are there any minimum performance standards required?
- Do the participants and, if appropriate, their parents, know what to expect?

2.3   Checking the Regulations

When beginning to plan a course the first point of reference should be the National Governing Body (NGB) regulations. These should give clear details of the number of hours needed to run the course. The hours given are often a minimum recommendation. Many tutors add additional hours to those recommended in order to permit more time:

- on syllabus topics
- on one to one tutorials
- on feedback from practical sessions
- on organised sessions to work on the logbook
- on additional opportunities for teaching/coaching
- on additional opportunities for tutor demonstration
- on additional opportunities for skill analysis
- to allow for unforeseen circumstances.

Some governing bodies also stipulate a maximum number of hours contact time per day. This is in the best interests of both tutors and candidates.

2.4 How Much Practical Time is Needed?

The majority of teacher/coach education courses include a practical element. This is probably not only the key issue when it comes to designing the course but, in terms of facilities, it is also likely to be the most expensive item. It is necessary to ascertain the maximum number of candidates to be enrolled on the course and assess the amount of practical time required and the availability of practical time. In many cases the NGB regulations will indicate the minimum amount of teaching/coaching each candidate needs to undertake. This means some calculations are required in order to identify the number of practical hours required. These requirements will be stipulated in the regulations.

Figure 3 - Considerations for calculating course/programme time - Practical

Factors related to practical work	Will be determined by the following:	Examples of possible allocations
1 Length of practical session	Regulations/syllabus; facility/space; ability of participants; candidate fatigue	1 hour
2 Number of candidates on the programme	Regulations/syllabus; facility/space; recruitment	12
3 Size of the practical facility/space	Facility/space	25 x 12 metres
4 Number of participants per candidate	Regulations/syllabus	12
5 Number of working stations	Facility/space; regulations/syllabus-participants per candidate	4
6 Number of candidates allocated to each working station, i.e., number of candidates divided by number of working stations	Factors 2, 3, 4 and 5	3
7 Length of working time per candidate per session	Regulations/syllabus	20 minutes
8 Total practical working per time per candidate	Regulations/syllabus	6 hours

9 Number of sessions needed to fulfil regulations demand per candidate, i.e., total regulation working time divided by session working time per candidate	Factors 7 and 8	18
10 Total practical working time for all candidates to meet requirements of the regulations, i.e., 3 candidates at each working station per session x 18 sessions	Factors 6, 7, 8 and 9	18 hours
11 Other factors to consider: (a) changeover times per session, non-working time, e.g., 5 minutes per session (b) other tutor led time, e.g., skill analysis and tutor demonstrations	Facility/space; professional organisation time, illness/absence Regulations/syllabus	1.5 hours 4 hours
Calculation for practical time	Factor 1 x Factor 10 Factor 11(a) Factor 11(b)	18 hours 1.5 hours 4 hours

Total practical time to meet the regulations within the constraints of the facility/space 23.5 hours

Figure 4 - Considerations for calculating course/programme time - Theory

Factors related to theory work	Will be determined by the following:	Some examples of possible allocations
1 Length of theory session	Facility/space; level of candidates; fatigue	1.5 hours
2 Size of the theory facility/space	Facility/space	8 x 6 metres
3 Total amount of theory time required to meet regulations/syllabus	Regulations/syllabus	21
4 Time for theory examination	Regulations/syllabus	1.75 hours
Calculation for theory time	Factor 3 Factor 4	21 hours 1.75 hours

Total theory time to meet the regulations within the constraintsof the facility/space 22.75 hours

Figure 5 - Summary of all totals of time

Total practical	23.5 hours
Total theory	22.75 hours
Session changeover/refreshment time between practical and theory sessions @ 15 mins per meeting x 18	4.5 hours
Total contact time for programme	50.75 hours

2.5   The Course Design Plan

Figure 6 – The decision-making process

Check regulations for number of hours needed.

Calculate number of practical hours required to cover minimum teaching/coaching requirements.

Check the cost of practical time, theory facilities and any additional staffing.

Decide on tutor fee.

Work out total costings to ensure course is viable.

Organise the practical time for teaching/coaching, skill analysis and tutor demonstrations.

Fit theory time around practical time remembering maximum contact hours.

Book lecture facilities and AVAs (if required).

Check the normal operating procedures and emergency action plans for the facilities.

Register course with NGB (if required).

Organise course publicity and circulate accordingly.

Arrange for course details to appear in relevant publications.

Organise participants for practical sessions.

Acknowledge applications and send out appropriate paperwork.

Plan content of course and methods of delivery.

2.6   First Shot Costings – is the course viable?

Before any publicity material can be produced the course will need to be priced and it is useful to try a "first shot costings" to get an indication of the viability.

Questions which will arise when costing the course are:
● what are the costs of such courses elsewhere?
● should the NGB assessment fee be included?
● should costs of resources (Logbook/portfolio and text book) be included?
● what will be the tutor's fee?
● should the participants pay?

Figure 7 - Example course costing for a NGB xxx Coach Certificate

Course Costings - NGB xxx Coach Certificate (Projection)

	Income	Expenditure
Candidate Fees (12 x £300.00)	£3600.00	
Facility Hire (24 hrs x £45.00)		£1080.00
Classroom Hire (30 hrs x £8.00)		£240.00
NGB Registration Fees (12 x £60.00)	£720.00	£720.00
Resource Materials (£10.00 per book)	£120.00	£120.00
Participants (£15.00 per participant)	£750.00	
Tutor (85 hrs x £20.00 per hour)		£1700.00
Postage		£60.00
Tutor expenses		£80.00
Logbooks/portfolios (£10.00 per log book)		£120.00
Administration		£100.00
	£5190.00	£4220.00

Costings are for maximum candidate numbers

Task 2 – Break even point

What is the break-even point in candidate numbers to ensure that expenditure in Figure 7 above does not exceed income?

Considerations when calculating costings:

- the cost of courses is variable and depends on the facilities to be used, the maximum number of candidates possible and the tutor fee. It is a fairly simple task to check costs by reading through the courses advertised in appropriate sporting journals

- if the assessment fee is not included in the price any publicity produced should make it clear that candidates will have to pay an additional fee on top of the course fee. This can be misleading and it is often easier to incorporate all of the possible costs at the first stage.

There are certain courses which have "required" resources, for example, the completion of a logbook/portfolio, whilst other resources are deemed "desirable" and will assist the candidate with their learning, for example, the appropriate textbook to support the course. As a tutor it is very useful to know that all candidates have both necessary and the desirable resources prior to arriving on the course. It means that the tutor can make reference to these materials during the course. Ensuring all candidates possess the logbook/portfolio prior to the course also provides the opportunity to guide them through the pre-course work. This both helps the candidate to be prepared for the course and also enables the tutor to complete a great deal of marking in advance of the course. The topic of pre-course action plans will be developed in more detail later in this section. There is also a discussion of the topic in Part 7, paragraph 7.5, *Pre-Course.*

The inclusion of assessment fees and resources in the costings gives a "no hidden extra" flavour to the course. Whilst this can be a useful marketing tool, it may also lead to problems in the future when it comes to isolating the assessment fee, especially if it has been absorbed into the coffers of a Local Authority, in order to send it to the NGB.

- **Tutor fees**

Technically, tutor rates are really related to the market forces and depend on the individual tutor's ability, experience and background. However, a NGB may sometimes recommend a tutor fee as guidance. When setting the tutor fee the following should be considered:

- The number of contact hours in the course.
- The number of non-contact hours in the course.
- The cost of travel to and from the venue.
- The production of handouts etc.
- Any accommodation costs which may be incurred.
- Any postage or other administration costs, e.g., telephone.
- The possibility of working unsocial hours.

The question of whether or not the participants who attend the course should pay will be discussed in more detail later.

2.7   Organising a Course

Organising a course as a tutor/organiser is made easier if a helper is available, particularly at the beginning. However, if the tutor is only responsible for the tutoring, it is important to guide the organiser through the course requirements stressing the importance of meeting the demands of the regulations. To reduce misunderstandings it is important to clearly set out on paper the allocation of responsibilities. Remember, the tutor is placing great reliance on the ability of an organiser who might be inexperienced and lacking a full understanding of the course requirements.

Figure 8 - Example roles and responsibilities document

Responsibilities of the Course Organiser
1. Booking facility
2. Establishing costings
3. Organising and circulating publicity
4. Registering course with the NGB (If appropriate)
5. Accepting and acknowledging bookings
6. Advising tutor of candidate information
7. Organising participants
8. Organising AVA and practical session equipment
9. Meeting candidates on arrival at first session
10. Organising any necessary refreshments
11. Liaising with participants and parents at practical sessions

The tutor will complete the following additional tasks:
1. Agreeing tutor fee with the course organiser
2. Advising the course organiser about the practical and theory hours time demands
3. Advising the course organiser of the numbers and abilities of any participants required for the practical work
4. Advising the course organiser of any AVA and other equipment requirements
5. Providing the course organiser with any pre-course information which might need sending out to candidates

The major responsibilities of the role of the tutor will be found by referring back to Part 1, paragraph 1.3, *The Job.*

2.8   Arranging the Facilities

Mention has already been made with regard to checking facility availability, but this was initially only related to the amount of time required in relation to the regulations. Previous reference has also been made to some of the other issues related to accessing practical times. Tutors should consider not only what is on offer but, also, the times of the availability and the length of each practical session possible within that time. Venues are often keen to offer their most unpopular times for the running of courses. It follows, therefore, that, if these are unpopular for the public, it will not be easy to find participants who will come to these sessions, e.g., a practical session for teaching/coaching children on a Sunday evening after 8.00pm.

The offers of large blocks of time in the practical environment without a break do not recognise the possible stress this can cause both candidates and tutor, and do not create an environment conducive to learning. A candidate may need to teach/coach many times in this one session. This does not permit time for reflection on what happened so that change could be effected. It also makes it very difficult for the tutor to provide any feedback which could have an immediate effect upon the next session taught.

When organising facilities it is also important for the tutor to consider the range of participants required within the course and the best way to access this range. For example, it might be more beneficial to attend a club session to utilise participants at a higher level on several occasions, rather than try to find participants of that level who will visit the main programme when needed. Another key consideration when selecting a facility is the availability of equipment and its suitability for the course being offered. Every effort should be made to ensure that candidates have the opportunity to experience a full range of equipment appropriate to the activity in which they are involved. Many facilities are sadly lacking in equipment.

A final comment concerning facilities is the provision of safety cover for the practical sessions. Every situation will differ, but it is by no means ideal for the tutor or the candidates to be providing the necessary safety cover, e.g., in the context of swimming, acting as life guarding cover for the pool. The requirements should be carefully checked and facilities should be given a clear indication of the course requirements in this area so that they can be provided and, if necessary, costed.

2.9 Arranging for the Participants

Having the appropriate number of participants to be taught/coached in the correct range of abilities is not an easy task, yet it is an essential part of running an effective course which meets the regulations. Often the task is left until last moment because it is seen to be less important. Tutors should keep reminding themselves that regulation demands are always important and that failure to meet them could mean that the course will be illegal in the eyes of the NGB. Because of the importance of local knowledge and contact, arranging for participants is one of the jobs which a tutor might pass on to a course organiser in the locality.

The two most common methods of organising a course (See also paragraph 2.10 below) with regard to participant provision are:

- utilising existing sessions where participants are already attending, e.g., a club or normal sessions
- organising special sessions and arranging participants accordingly

Both systems inevitably have pros and cons. Using existing sessions means that the participants are already attending and, inevitably, this means that there is less organisation involved. However, difficulties could arise in ensuring that the right range and number of participants are available. Another advantage of using existing sessions is that the facility might already be paid for, thus reducing costs for the candidates. Tutors must also be sensitive to the existing arrangements with regard to teachers/coaches and helpers who normally take these sessions. Another matter to negotiate is that existing sessions might have to be reorganised to take account of the demands of the regulations for the course. Organising special sessions means participants have to be recruited but this does permit the right level of participants, in terms of ability, to be found. It also allows for the opportunity to charge the participants.

No matter what system is adopted it is essential that all participants and, if appropriate, their parents, know what the course is about and that there is likely to be a break in normal routines whilst it is running. This can often be "sold" to club members and classes as a means of increasing the future quality of service to their customers, i.e., the parents and other members.

2.10 Organising the Sessions

Utilising existing sessions – An example of this might be by making use of:
- a club session
- a sports development session
- organised teaching/coaching sessions, e.g., school classes.

It might even need to be a combination of these examples in order to cover the range of abilities and participants necessary to achieve the qualification, e.g., children and adults, novice and high level performers.

Special sessions - If special sessions are organised participants will need to be recruited from a number of sources:
- Existing sessions at the facility.
- Participants who belong to local clubs.
- Participants from schools, particularly those who do not have many sporting opportunities.
- Contact through advertising.

Of course, there is no reason why participants cannot be accessed using both methods and, ultimately, bring out the best of both worlds.

Should the participants pay for the practical sessions?
As suggested earlier, when setting up a course, tutors and organisers often debate this question. Tutors are often concerned about charging participants to be taught/coached by inexperienced candidates. Like most things in life, there are pros and cons for both methods.

- **Pros (paying for sessions)**
  - Participants make a commitment and are more likely to attend.
  - Participants feel that it will be worth their while if they pay for it.
  - It provides additional income which can help to offset costs and often reduce the course fee for candidates.
  - It is much easier to check the range of participants enrolling.
  - The number of participants will be known prior to the course commencing and allow the planning of more effective practical sessions.

- **Pros (free sessions)**
  - The candidates' inexperience is less of a concern.
  - The sessions are open to all - not only those who can afford it.
  - Something for nothing is always an attractive proposition.
  - It is often easier to obtain large numbers of willing volunteers.
  - The structure of the sessions can be organised to suit the needs of the course most effectively.
  - There is no pressure to offer a specific session since parents, if properly briefed, will not expect participants to have a normal lesson.

There will never be one right or wrong answer to the question of whether or not participants pay. The right answer will be the one which suits the situation and location of each particular course. Charging a nominal fee has been a successful method although, sometimes, the participants take the view that they have paid and, therefore, they can chose when they want to attend. The essential feature is that the enrolment information gives a clear indication of the nature of the programme and allows them to make informed decisions prior to enrolling.

An alternative view on the issue of the candidates being inexperienced is that because they are trying to gain a qualification they will be working very hard and often display a highly motivated attitude to the teaching/coaching process because their own result will depend on it. Whilst participants and their parents recognise the candidates are inexperienced, they also recognise that the course tutor is constantly monitoring them. As a result, participants who enrol for one course will often constantly reappear on future courses.

2.11   Further Factors in the Design and Organisation of a Course

The nature and shape of the programme will be influenced by the result of addressing a number of questions related to the approach to the delivery of the sessions.

The facility requirements for the theory work – These are usually much simpler to provide, much more readily available and can probably be fitted around the other aspects of planning. These can be addressed by considering the following:

- How long should a theory session run without a break?
- What is the shortest possible time allocation for a theory session?
- Are there times of the day which are more suited to theory sessions e.g., when there are minimal distractions; when the candidates are not too tired?
- Will the theory sessions provide knowledge appropriate to the practical sessions which follow?
- What are the implications should it not be possible for theory sessions to proceed practical work?

The underpinning knowledge needed to become an effective teacher/coach is essential and it would be unfortunate to find that a candidate was weak in this area because the course had been poorly designed and organised.

Figure 9 – Basic planning process for theory sessions

Identify learning outcomes

↓

Determine methods of learning and associated activities

↓

Production of session plan

The facility requirements for the practical work – The smooth running of the practical sessions relies heavily on good forward planning at the design and organisation stage. This aspect of the course often proves to be one of the most difficult planning tasks for a tutor to undertake. At the practical sessions there will usually be a range of different individuals to co-ordinate, candidates, participants and observers, all needing to know where to go and what to do, especially during the first session. There will also be the need to ensure that all candidates have been provided with the opportunity to teach/coach over the full range abilities of the syllabus demands, as well as enabling them to demonstrate their ability to teach/coach the appropriate range of skills/physical conditioning techniques related to the sport itself.

When designing the practical programme consider implications for:

- **Rotation** – To ensure that each candidate covers the required range of abilities during the course.

- **Number of Stations** – The number of working stations feasible in relation to the space available, the number of participants, the number of candidates and the tutor observation/assessment which need to be carried out.

- **Participants Required** - The numbers and abilities of the participants as determined by the regulations. Part 2, paragraphs 2.9, *Arranging for the Participants* and 2.10, *Organising the Sessions*, discussed this topic in some detail.

- **Source of Participants** - Where will the participants be found? Again, paragraphs 2.9 and 2.10, made reference to this issue.

- **Range of Abilities** - A local club might be an ideal source for the experienced, more able participant but, perhaps, not appropriate for providing the novice participant. Again, paragraphs 2.9 and 2.10 referred to this in detail.

- **Assessment Requirements** – The importance attached to assessment means that it has implications for the design and organisation stage of the process. Planning the *who, when* and *what* of assessments not only ensures that none of the assessment objectives are missed but, also, that provision is made at the design stage for assessments to occur.

Task 3 – Planning for assessment

Who is assessed when?

An organisation plan for practical sessions is detailed below. The plan allows for all 12 candidates on the course to experience 30 minutes coaching during the 1.5 hours time allocation (candidates are indicated by a capital letter). Note that over the 6 practical sessions shown each candidate has an opportunity to coach a different level of ability.

By the end of these sessions each candidate will have been assessed twice. Using the information given outline an assessment plan to ensure that this will happen. Indicate by highlighting the candidate on the organisation plan.

Whilst doing this exercise take into account the following:
- The level of participant being coached.
- How many candidates might be assessed at the same time.

Session 1	9.00am	9.30am	10.00am
Station 1 (new participants)	A	E	I
Station 2 (improvers - level 1)	B	F	J
Station 3 (improvers - level 2)	C	G	K
Station 4 (advanced performers)	D	H	L

Session 2	9.00am	9.30am	10.00am
Station 1 (new participants)	L	D	H
Station 2 (improvers - level 1)	I	A	E
Station 3 (improvers - level 2)	J	B	F
Station 4 (advanced performers)	K	C	G

Session 3	9.00am	9.30am	10.00am
Station 1 (new participants)	G	K	C
Station 2 (improvers - level 1)	H	L	D
Station 3 (improvers - level 2)	E	I	A
Station 4 (advanced performers)	F	J	B

Session 4	9.00am	9.30am	10.00am
Station 1 (new participants)	B	F	J
Station 2 (improvers - level 1)	C	G	K
Station 3 (improvers - level 2)	D	H	L
Station 4 (advanced performers)	A	E	I

Session 5	9.00am	9.30am	10.00am
Station 1 (new participants)	I	A	E
Station 2 (improvers - level 1)	J	B	F
Station 3 (improvers - level 2)	K	C	G
Station 4 (advanced performers)	L	D	H

Session 6	9.00am	9.30am	10.00am
Station 1 (new participants)	H	L	D
Station 2 (improvers - level 1)	E	E	A
Station 3 (improvers - level 2)	F	J	B
Station 4 (advanced performers)	G	K	C

2.12 Course Design and the Use of Distance Learning

Many tutors choose to employ a system of pre-course tuition (See also Part 7, paragraph 7.5, *Pre-Course*). This can be achieved through a form of distance learning which helps the tutor to prepare the candidates adequately for the course ahead, as well as freeing up the tutor so that a greater degree of one to one contact becomes possible later on. The benefits for the candidates are considerable in that they begin their learning in a guided manner and arrive better prepared for the start of the course. Other applications of this system will be developed in Part 7, paragraph 7.4, *Postal Work and Distance Learning*.

Work via distance learning prior to the course is an excellent way of ensuring the candidate arrives at the course ready to embark on the more practical aspects. It is also a good way of developing a tutor/candidate relationship at the earliest possible opportunity.

Part 3

The Detailed Planning

3.1 Making the Arrangements

Once the planning and organising stages are complete the tutor needs to consider the detailed implications for getting the show on the road.

- **Booking the venue** - Requirements for booking venues will differ from facility to facility. Some will have formalised procedures with a hire agreement to be completed, whilst others will need to be sent a letter of confirmation. Facility booking should always be done in writing and the tutor should keep a copy. This is very important because many facilities work on a shift basis with different staff taking responsibility for bookings. A verbal booking can easily be forgotten, or not recorded, and the staff on duty on the day the course begins may have no knowledge of the booking. The confirmation letter is essential, as is the "on-the-day" phone call to make sure everything is OK.

  Sometimes the course is held in different facilities, e.g., practical and theory maybe in different places. If this is the case a letter should be sent to each place to confirm the arrangements. When sending a confirmation letter it is also useful to state all the requirements for the course, e.g., equipment, staffing etc. It is important to be precise, e.g., ordering an overhead projector (OHP) does not necessarily mean that a screen will also appear with it! These details need to be confirmed in writing to the organiser if such duties are to be one of the responsibilities for that person. Never assume that the organiser will know what is needed. It is also advisable to follow this through and check that the requests have been carried out.

- **Candidate letter of confirmation** – Confirm candidates' applications as they are received and provide them with any additional information. This is likely to include some, or all, of the following:

  - Start date, time and venue.
  - Details of timing and venue of each session.
  - Outline timetable.
  - Textbooks required.
  - What the candidates should bring.
  - Appropriate dress for the practical sessions.
  - Any pre-course work required.

It may also include some of the general information from the syllabus and course regulations, and a copy of the regulations. The early provision of this type of information can help to get the course moving more effectively at the first session.

Figure 10 - Example letter of confirmation to candidates

Tutor's address…and contact details

Date

Candidate Name & Address

Dear xxx

NGB Teacher/Coach Certificate - Level 2

Thank you for your application for the NGB Teacher/Coach Certificate-Level 2 at xxx Leisure Centre from Saturday, xx August, 1999 to Saturday, xx August. A place has now been reserved for you.

Please find enclosed a receipt acknowledging payment of your course and assessment fees. I will arrange to deliver the xxxtextbook to you in the next two weeks. In the meantime you should obtain a copy of the logbook/portfolio which goes with this course. If you require further advice my contact details are at the head of this letter.

Below are the timings for the course and an indication of what you should bring with you:

Start Time: 9.00am each day
Finish Time: 5.30pm each day
Lunch: 12.30pm - 1.15pm (lunch will not be provided)
Requirements: Pens and paper for theory sessions
                 Suitable dress for the practical sessions (shorts, t-shirt, tracksuit)
                 Logbook/portfolio
                 Whistle
                 Pre-requisite certificate number
                 Packed lunch

The logbook/portfolio requires you to complete some work prior to the start of the course. I have attached a pre-course work action plan to assist you with this. Please contact me if you have any questions with regard to completing the work.

Finally, I have enclosed an outline timetable for you information. I look forward to meeting with you on Saturday, xx August, at 8.45am
Yours sincerely

Course Tutor

3.2 Pre-Course Briefing

It is very useful to have a pre-course briefing. With the first level ofteaching/coaching courses this enables the tutor to cover some of the theory work prior to the candidates being expected to teach/coach. One of the difficulties experienced at this level will be the necessity for candidates to have some understanding of teaching/coaching and skills/techniques prior to the first session. Clearly it is not possible to tell them everything, but it is worthwhile covering some basic points prior to the first practical session. Additionally, it should be remembered that the time availability for the course might mean that the first session is practical, anyway. (See also, Part 7, paragraph 7.5, *Pre-Course*).

At the higher levels of qualification the pre-course briefing will allow the tutor to give a thorough explanation of the course requirements and examine in detail any paperwork to be completed as part of the course, e.g., a logbook/portfolio. Furthermore it allows specific tasks, which should be completed before the main core of the course, to be discussed. It may also provide an opportunity for collecting any completed work for marking. This will lighten the future load for both tutor and candidates.

3.3 Pre-Course Work/Action Plan

Many NGB teacher/coach education courses now include the completion of a logbook/portfolio as part of the course/assessment. Often there is work to be completed prior to the start of the course but, even when this is clearly laid out, candidates do not always do it. Some candidates simply do not read any of the logbook/portfolio, assuming that it will only be utilised as part of the course. Candidates have been known to arrive at the first session of the course with the logbook/portfolio unopened – even still cling wrapped! Drawing attention to the main pre-course requirements in the confirmation letter is one way of reducing this problem. Whilst this is helpful it still means candidates are working with little guidance and that the marking of the pre-course and on-course work during the course still remains a considerable task. (See also, Part 7, paragraph 7.5, *Pre-Course*).

A better solution is to offer tutor support before the course begins by setting a plan for achieving and returning work prior to the actual start of the course. This assists the candidate which, inevitably, assists the tutor. Not only can work be marked prior to the course, but candidates' strengths and weaknesses can be identified and desperately needed, beneficial feedback provided. If the candidates progress well they may be able to complete additional work prior to the course, making the on-course workload far less stressful. Even if there is no pre-course work specified in the logbook/portfolio, it may still be helpful to adopt this system, particularly if the course is of an intensive or semi-intensive nature. The work can be quite considerable and it is a much easier task for the candidate to complete it gradually rather than leaving it until the last minute.

Figure 11 - Example 1 Pre-course work Action Plan

NGB Teacher/Coach Certificate2 – Pre-course work Action Plan

It is important to understand that the NGB Teacher/Coach Certificate 2 is part of a process of continuing development. This means that there is an expectation that you will have continued to develop your own skills after completing the NGB Teacher/Coach Certificate1.

The work you complete in your logbook/portfolio is to help you complete the NGB Teacher/Coach Certificate2 successfully and every effort should be made to learn from it, not just do it.

In order to assist you with the pre-course aspects of the NGB Teacher/Coach Certificate2, tutor support is offered from now until the course begins. Follow the guidance given in each pre-course work pack (this is the first), complete the tasks accordingly and forward them to me before the date on the front of the pack. If you have difficulty in completing the task please contact me.

As soon as I receive this pack I will forward the next one to you etc.

Course Tutor

Work Programme
Pre-course work - Part 1

1.   Read sub section 5 on page 7 of section V

2.   Read chapter 4 in xxxtextbook. This will help you to complete some of the following work.

3.   Complete a Scheme of Work for a beginners group of 8 participants aged 5 - 7. The scheme of work should cover a minimum of six sessions.

     If you currently teach a group of beginners similar to the one above, base your scheme of work around this group. If you are not teaching a group such as this complete your scheme of work on a hypothetical basis.

4.   Answer questions 1-7 and 24-29. These can be found in section V page 20.

5.   Read chapter 12 in xxxtextbook. This will help you to complete some of the following work

6.   Using the analysis form to be found in section X of your logbook/portfolio, complete two analyses.

7.   Send in your work to me as soon as it is completed.

General

If you complete any additional session plans and evaluations between now and the course starting please put them into section XIII of your logbook/portfolio and number the pages accordingly, e.g., 20.1, 20.2 etc.

Figure 12 - Example 2 Pre-course work Action Plan

NGB Teacher/Coach Certificate3 - Pre-course work Action Plan

The action plan detailed below is intended as an aid to assist you in planning your work in a structured and progressive manner prior to attending the NGB Teacher/Coach Certificate3 Course.

As you will see, there are times when completed work needs to be forwarded to the me for checking and marking (The items on the action plan marked *). Please send the work, along with a stamped addressed envelope to the address shown above. I will then return it with any appropriate comments or contact you by telephone if I feel it is necessary.

Task	Explanation	To be completed by
Organise some teaching/coaching practice	If you are not already actively teaching/ coaching it is important that you organise some with a club immediately. Ideally, this should be in the situation in which you will work for in the post-course logbook/portfolio activity. Any practice is better than none, so, even if it is only looking after a small group under the guidance of another coach, this will still prove useful.	
* Section 2 Personal Details & Personal Development Plan	Fill in the Curriculum Vitae with reference to your sport. Read the page on Planning for Personal Development and complete your Personal Development Plan. In order to avoid confusion, if you have nothing to enter at a particular point, write "n/a".	
* Section 3 Timetable of teaching/ coaching commitments	Complete this timetable in accordance with your current teaching/coaching commitment.	
* Section 3 Participant profiles (10 Required)	Begin to gather information relating to the participants you are teaching/coaching. You may not be able to complete all details on the Participants' Profile Sheets at the moment, so these should be added to as more information becomes available.	
* Section 3 Cyclic Training Plan	Read the information on *Cyclic Training Plans* in *Chapter 8 in xxxtextbook*. Prepare a cyclic training plan related to the participants you are teaching/coaching.	

3.4 Registration

Whilst there is often a requirement for courses to be registered with the NGB prior to commencement, this process will, inevitably, vary. In some cases the NGB might play the role of course organiser and set up the courses. In other cases recognised tutors will be permitted to set up courses themselves, or in conjunction with a local organiser. In this case the registration with the NGB is a means of it being aware of the teaching/coaching courses being held nationally. There might also be a need to appoint some form of Internal Verifier/Moderator to monitor the quality of assessment on the course. (See also, Part 5, paragraph 5.2, *The Assessment Process – What is involved?* and paragraph 5.3, *The Assessment – How is it done?*)

There are usually some basic requirements when registering a course:
- Course details.
- Breakdown of time.
- Theory timetable.
- Practical organisation.
- Possible number of candidates.

All these items will be needed at a later stage and should have been completed as part of the planning and organising, so supplying this information should not be a problem. The NGB may have a minimum recommended time for registration of a course, e.g., 28 days prior to the course commencing, but the earlier the registration of the course the easier will be the checking of the details, the ironing out of any problems and the appointment of an Internal Verifier/Moderator. Registration may also be a useful marketing tool as many potential teachers/coaches will contact the NGB to ascertain the availability of courses.

3.5   Marketing the Course

Once the planning and organising stages have been completed the course will need effective marketing. If this is done badly all the previous hard work will have been wasted.

The key aspects of marketing the course are:
- when to market?
- how to market?
- where to market?
- what is the target group?

When to market
Some people argue that a product can never be marketed too early. This might be true if the marketing can be maintained throughout the period up to the course, but there is always a danger of early marketing losing its initial appeal. The type of course and the number of candidates required will often influence when the process begins and the methods to be used. Some courses, usually of the shorter variety with a minimal time commitment, often receive the most applications quite late because the candidates will not have to make changes in their personal arrangements in order to attend. The longer courses, in particular the intensive versions, often require candidates to rearrange their normal day to day routines, perhaps even arranging to take leave from work etc. In these cases there is a need for courses to be marketed early to allow candidates the time to make the appropriate arrangements. Any course which includes an element of pre-course work should also be marketed as early as possible. The promoting and publicising of the course should begin as soon as the planning stages are complete and alerting potential candidates to the likelihood of a course and opening of a list of names and addresses for future mailing will pay dividends.

How to market
A range of options might include:
- producing a flyer
- producing a poster
- advertising in the appropriate journal.
- advising the NGB

- word of mouth
- through your sports teaching/coaching association
- through local sports centres
- through local clubs
- internet.

Inevitably, the best approach is to consider using a variety of methods.

Where to Market

This has a very close link with "How to Market". Clearly if the chosen method is to produce flyers, careful thought then needs to be given to the most appropriate places for them to be circulated. An inappropriate choice of location for marketing tools, such as flyers and posters, not only means that the target group might be missed, but time and money will have been wasted. The figure below gives an indication of the most likely places and people which might be targeted.

Figure 13 – Possible marketing contacts

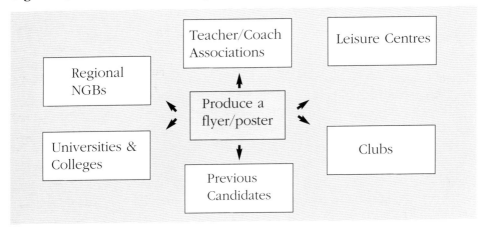

3.6   Planning the Individual Sessions – The detail

Introduction
In Part 2, paragraph 2.11, *Further Factors in the Design and Organisation of a Course,* Figure 9, some basic ideas and principles of outline planning were discussed in relation to the nature and shape of the programme, and the implications for this at the planning and organisation stage. What now needs to be addressed is the detailed planning of the content of the presentations.

Gather the data
The course syllabus will provide information which will help identify the data that needs to be gathered.

This will include:

- the aims and objectives of the course
- the learning outcomes of the course
- the range and level of the material to be used
- the broad headings upon which the presentations will be based
- the key texts which support the course to be delivered
- checking other sources for appropriate information, e.g.,
  - other sport specific textbooks
  - articles which appear in sport specific journals
  - articles from other countries' sporting journals
  - other tutors within the sport
  - other teaches/coaches in the sport
  - data of a generic nature related to teaching/coaching
  - courses of a generic nature related to teaching/coaching
  - NGB textbooks specific to the teacher/coach education programmes
  - the Internet.

Whilst tutors should be familiar with the course texts used by the candidates, they should also try to access information from as wide a range of sources as possible in order to ensure that they can make their material both interesting and up to date.

Identify Learning Outcomes

It is important to know what the candidates are expected to learn, both from the course as a whole and as a series of outcomes on the way. The setting out of aims and objectives will enable the tutor to determine whether or not the outcomes have been successful. This is known as identifying learning outcomes. Essentially, the learning outcomes will be based on the course syllabus, although, sometimes, learning outcomes will be related to the syllabus indirectly by referring to underpinning knowledge and skills learned from previous levels of work. With learning outcomes clearly identified the selection of materials and methods becomes a more focused activity.

Selecting the range

This has lots of implications for starting and end points.

The range will be influenced by:
- what? (Content of the presentation and course syllabus)
- why? (Reason why candidates need it)
- how? (Method of delivery)
- who? (The audience and its needs)
- where? (The environment such as classroom or practical area)
- when? (Time of day and duration)
- the level of materials
- the selection of materials in general.

A wide range of material will have been used when gathering data for session notes, so careful selection is very important. Delivering material at the wrong level can have serious repercussions on most candidates and may not only result in lack of understanding and loss of confidence, but it will also leave them ill prepared to teach/coach. More worryingly it could actually demotivate them.

The outline programme

Setting out the outline programme, including a consideration of the content and method, in a logical sequence leads to a structured approach to the whole programme and the ability to identify other items which will contribute to the effective running of the course.

Figure 14 - Example outline planning for theory sessions

Time	Session	Method	Candidate participation	Outcomes	Method of assessment
09.00	Introduction	Briefing	Questions	Knowledge	Candidate behaviour and responses
10.00	Anatomy	Lecture	Questions	Knowledge	Sheet for Q & A
11.00	Break				
11.15	Session planning	Lesson	Desk exercise	Competence to produce a session plan	Assessment of plan by tutor/assessor
12.15	Yearly plans	Syndicates /Groups back	Group work and report	Competence to produce yearly plans meeting criteria	Assessment of plan by tutor/assessor

It is not possible to plan exactly either how each session will proceed or the exact responses of the candidates. However, well planned sessions will provide better overall control and permit the achievement of the learning outcomes through a variety of methods within the time allocated. The information derived from this type of exercise will assist in the identification of possible delivery methods together with the relevant AVA and the other equipment needed at various times during the programme.

The selection of audio visual aids (AVAs)
A possible range of AVAs for the classroom environment includes:

- overhead projector (OHP) and screen (Walls as screens do not offer a "professional" image)
- slide projector
- wipe boards or chalkboards
- handout
- textbook
- video and audio resources
- posters and charts
- desk top computers
- personal demonstrations by the tutor.

It must be remembered that Audio Visual Aids (AVAs) are a learning aid which should supplement the session, not dominate it. Remember the phrase "death by overhead" when considering the use of AVAs. There is no doubt that AVAs, used in an appropriate manner, can greatly enhance a session. They give candidates the opportunity to use two senses, sight and sound, the combination of which create a powerful learning experience. Combining the balance between two or three different AVAs within one theory session is likely to maintain the candidates' interest without overloading and confusing them. They should be carefully selected to both support the presentations and be appropriate for the candidates' needs. Marking or highlighting presentation notes where visual materials are intended to be used is a valuable way of ensuring that effective use is made of the AVA material.

Timing

Sessions need to be timed accurately to ensure:

- that the syllabus is covered in the appropriate time
- the interest of the candidates is maintained
- that a good role model is provided for the candidates in their own work.

Session notes should provide an indication of the time to be spent on each aspect of the presentation. This will only be a guide, but it will allow the identification of timing issues and any problems of possible overrun. This can then be addressed prior to the session so that a strategy to deal with it can be implemented sooner rather than later.

Questions

Inevitably questioning will need to be incorporated into the sessions. Methods of questioning were highlighted in Part 1, paragraph 1.6, *Dealing with Questions*. Questioning, in whatever form, adds additional time to the any session and provision for this needs to be made when preparing session notes. Time should also be allocated in all sessions for candidate led questions. Carefully designed presentation notes, packed with interesting information, should also be accompanied by a selection of prepared answers to some of the most common questions asked by candidates.

Candidate support materials

The preparation of session notes and data gathering will involve searches for useful articles, textbooks etc. Often these will provide excellent support material for candidates. Be prepared to provide additional information at the end of sessions to show how candidates can enhance their current knowledge, e.g., a simple handout referencing certain chapters in a textbook or articles in a journal. Referencing support materials is a good method of ensuring that those candidates who are keen and eager for knowledge are able to follow up their interest independently.

3.7   Preparing the Session Notes

Whilst Part 2, paragraph 2.11, *Further Factors in the Design and Organisation of a Course*, briefly introduced the topic of preparing session notes, it is so important that a more detailed treatment is now offered. Many painstaking presenters have risen to speak, only to find their notes more of a hindrance than help! Whatever notes are used they should be designed to serve as an *aide-memoire* only and not a complete text for reading word for word. They should not be learned as script for a play!

Notes can be formatted in a number of ways:
- as index cards
- as paper sheets
- as memory maps.

Tutors find many different ways of structuring their material and allocating their time in order to cover all the points they plan to make. Below are two examples.

Figure 15 - Example memory map

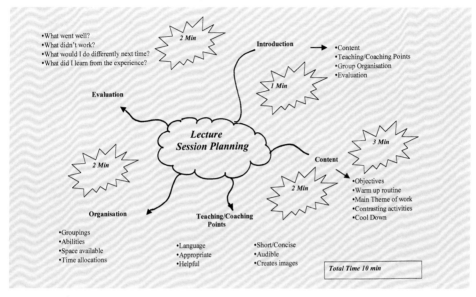

Figure 16 - Example index cards

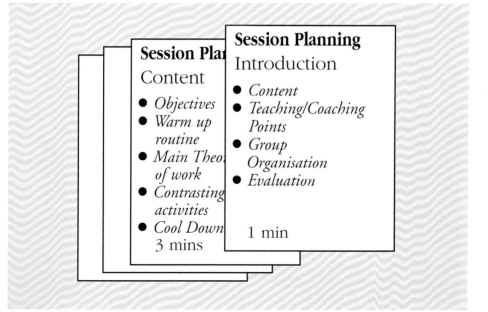

- **Summary - Preparing Session Notes**

  Any preparation will be made easier if a structured process is followed:
  - **Identify learning outcomes** – see Part 3, paragraph 3.6, *Planning the Individual Sessions – The detail.*
  - **Define the main headings under which the points will be made** – see Part 3, paragraph 3.7, *Preparing the Session Notes,* Figures 15 and 16.
  - **Place in a logical sequence** – see Part 3, as above.
  - **Assemble appropriate information** – see *Gather the Data,* paragraph 3.6, *Planning the Individual Sessions – The detail.*
  - **Note particular supporting illustrative examples, anecdotes or quotes**

- **Ensure that the balance and points for emphasis are right** – Identify the degree of importance of the facts and divide them into three categories:
  - **Vital** - must be included.
  - **Useful** - should be included.
  - **Interesting** - may be included if time permits.

- **Be aware of time constraints – do not try to cover too much**

- **Review the use of the preparation notes**

  Ensuring that the notes are prepared in a way that makes them user friendly, i.e., to the presenter. They should be designed as rapid reminders for use *at a glance* so that the flow of what is being said is unbroken.

  Considerations for the use of the notes are:
  - where will the notes be placed?
  - will it be possible to read the notes easily?
  - will colour for headings and highlighting key points will make it easier?
  - should the notes be written in block capitals?
  - would double spacing help?
  - how will the pages or cards be numbered to avoid possible confusion?

- how will timing be checked?
- what visual materials will be used?
- when will the visuals be used?
- how will the use of the visuals be highlighted on the notes?
- will candidate tasks be used?
- when will candidate tasks be used?

It should be remembered that tutoring is a two way process, and the involvement of the learners in their own learning, through the use of tasks and discussion, is a very effective way of developing understanding and attitude. This has become known as the teacher/coach centred approach to tutoring and, inevitably, involves a greater degree of planning than is perhaps necessary for the more formal, didactic, presentation. Poorly planned and badly designed tasks can result in little or no learning.

- **Practice the presentation**
  Inexperienced tutors might find it helpful to rehearse, possibly with the use of a tape recorder. This will help:
  - to iron out any potential problems regarding notes, visuals, unclear explanations
  - to become familiar with the planned progression
  - to build up self-confidence in the use of the material.

- **Consider the method of delivery** - see Part 1, paragraph 1.5, *Creating a Learning Environment*, and Part 4, paragraph, 4.4, *Delivering the Theory.*

Figure 17 - Example of the production of a session plan (Theory)

This example suggests how the topic might be approached using session planning as a focus for a group of candidates. It identifies the methods to be utilised, the learning outcomes and the possible time allocations for each part of the session.

Aim   To equip candidates with the knowledge and skills to plan, conduct and evaluate a session and a series of sessions

Syllabus Item   Recording & evaluating:
- of personal effectiveness
- of the success of the session and the series
- the individual improvement of participants through the use of relevant records

Outcomes   Evaluation and record keeping:
- self-evaluation of sessions
- evaluations of a scheme of work
- keeping appropriate records and making use of them
- effecting change as a result of evaluations

Introduction (3 mins)

A session plan has two functions:
- it is a strategy for teaching
- it is a series of cues to be used during the lesson

The session plan can be divided into two key sections:

- initial information
- the main theme of the plan

Development (45 mins)

- **Methods**
  - **Brainstorming** - What can be recorded in a teaching/coaching (5 mins)   environment which may be useful?

  - **Group Questioning** - Go through answers and identify what each item can (5 mins)   tell us?

- **Group Lecture** - Part of recording information may also be evaluating the
  (15 mins)   performer/session/plan/self
  - Evaluation assists with future planning.
  - Evaluation gives opportunities to re-plan

- **Group Work** - On flip chart sheet - write a list of what a useful evaluation
  (10 mins)   of a lesson should include
  - Discuss lists

- **Case Study** - Set a scenario for candidates to work on in pairs
  (10 mins)   Session plan plus evaluation and short explanation
  - How can the next session be more successful?

Summary - Record appropriate information
(5 mins)
- Evaluate self, participants, session, and plan
- Set an action plan

Questions/Further discussion (7 mins)

Tutor Requirements	**Total time = 60 mins**

Flip chart pad	Overhead transparencies(OHTs)	Logbook evaluation sheet
Marker pens	Case study	

Part 4

Running the Course

4.1   Building the Team and Setting the Scene

Building the team

To run a successful course or sports workshop the tutor needs the full cooperation of the candidates and the collective knowledge and skills of all who take part. Engaging the candidates' own learning styles means that learning is maximized. This will be achieved by creating concrete experiences allowing all course members, including the tutor, to take part in the activities. Where the event is based solely on the delivery of technical sport specific knowledge, then involving the candidates might become less important and the information can be presented with minimal candidate input and interaction, using, for example, the lecture method.

Key aspects of team building are:
- introducing candidates to each other and bonding via pre-designed activities
- briefing the team on course objectives and outcomes, regulations, safety etc
- giving candidates a clear view of the task ahead of them
- recognising the collective competence together with the training needs
- giving feedback on performance
- motivating the team
- minimising conflicts and building trust
- recognising and rewarding success.

Considerations

When a tutor runs the course there may be aspects of the syllabus which are of a particularly sensitive nature. An immediate example which springs to mind is the issue of child protection and good teaching/coaching practice. This area of any syllabus is of increasing importance and the raising of awareness amongst teachers/coaches is a priority.

When dealing with issues of a sensitive nature the tutor needs to consider very carefully the approach to the topic which may raise personal emotions in a variety of different forms. It could be a personal experience or, perhaps, a situation, which the teacher/coach has observed from a distance, which may bring back some difficult memories. When setting the scene prior to beginning a presentation/discussion on such a topic the tutor needs an initial principles statement which will help to establish some boundaries and behaviour guidelines.

Figure 18 - Principles Statement - Ch

- Very emotive subject
  - feel free to exclude yourself from any d...
    uncomfortable in any way
  - feel free to leave the room at any stage in t...
    and return when you are ready

- If you wish to discuss experiences or examples pl... ...re anonymity
  is maintained

- Everybody's input, however small, is valuable. All input should be valued
  by the group

- Maintain confidentiality. The discussions which take place should end as
  we leave the classroom

These types of opening statements help candidates to feel at ease and it is very important that the tutor then abides by this principles statement.

The way a tutor introduces a topic of a sensitive nature is also very important. An empathetic approach is often needed and the tutor's choice of words in the introduction can set the scene in a sensitive and understanding manner. For example, using the issue of child protection again, introducing the topic by first looking at good teaching/coaching practice guidelines begins to raise the key issues gradually and will lead into child protection and then child abuse. To begin the topic using a statement such as *"What is child abuse?"* or *"What do you understand by the term 'Child Abuse?'"* could leave candidates feeling very vulnerable. This could lead to a candidate being unable to deal with his/her emotions in an appropriate manner or even unwillingness to respond at all.

Not only do topics of a sensitive nature need careful planning prior to the course but, also, the tutor needs to be able to respond to the group in the most appropriate manner. This is likely to vary from group to group and must be dealt with accordingly. There is a reference above to the need for anonymity. Not only is it important to apply it in the context of sensitive issues, but it is also important in the context of being professional in general. Discourage candidates from naming people, centres, clubs, etc. It is one thing to say, *es...*", but quite a different matter to name names. To discuss ~~eople~~ople or places would be quite unprofessional.

~~ing~~ the scene

You only get one chance to make a first impression – don't blow it!

The single most destructive element in any learning situation is fear. It is, therefore, vital that the tutor minimises this at the very start of the course by giving all candidates a clear view of what they will be doing, the demands that will be placed upon them, and the support that will be available. Once they have a full, unambiguous understanding of how the event will run they are less likely to be distracted by tension.

It is the tutor's responsibility to create an environment in which candidates feel secure and confident in the tutor's competence. They also need to know that they are in a supportive climate which will maximise their learning. If, however, candidates feel that the course is only being used to assess their current competence and, because of this, they feel isolated, they will withdraw and fear is likely to blot out any learning.

The beginning of any course is a 'moment of truth' and a defining event.

Tutors should:
- introduce themselves
- establish ground rules for the course, such as:
  - treating each other with respect
  - only one person speaking at a time
  - starting and finishing on time
  - supporting each other
  - speaking up if the session is becoming non-productive
  - not re-inventing, re-organising or generally decrying the NGB
  - giving an assurance that the tutor will not embarrass any candidate and will be as supportive as possible

- brief candidates on:
  - the facilities available
  - health and Safety aspects, e.g., fire exits, toilets
  - course content and timetable
  - assessment processes
  - performance criteria and NGB assessment criteria
  - feedback methods and confidentiality
  - when they will have an opportunity to ask questions
  - the importance of mutual respect and the need for trust
  - the importance of having some fun along the way!

4.2. Getting to Know Each Other

Introductions

At the start of the course it is essential that the individuals get to know and trust each other and adequate time should be given over to the introductions. There is a tendency for individuals to distrust strangers and fear the unknown. If these two barriers can be removed early on there is a greater probability of a successful outcome. The key challenge at the start of a course is for everyone to be known, and to be called by their preferred name.

This can be achieved in a number of ways:
- Through presentations by individuals.
- By the use of "Ice breakers".
- Through "Team build" and informal activities.

Individual presentations can be informal, letting them talk about themselves for a few minutes, or more formalised whereby the tutor sets the agenda and time scale. For example, they might be asked to talk for 5 minutes about where they live, their family and their current job. A useful aspect can be to also ask them personally what they wish to get out of the course. Remember, some candidates might feel very threatened by being invited to make an individual presentation.

"Ice Breakers" are common methods of getting candidates to interact with each other in pairs and mingling on some data gathering activity, e.g., ask candidates to break up into pairs and in 5 minutes learn something about each other (in specific areas set by the tutor) and ask them to present each other to the rest of the group.

Team building activities involve setting a task for the whole group or smaller groups causing them to interact with each other. Some element of competition with a prize might inject some fun into the event. Informal activities can include tea breaks, a drink at the bar or a casual walk. Although the activities are informal in themselves, the tutor needs to 'engineer' the event and set time constraints. The latter point is particularly important. The amount of interaction during these informal periods is clearly less predictable, and the wise tutor will use all of the above to a greater or lesser extent. The final challenge is for the tutor to learn every name on the course in the first thirty minutes of it starting. This is less demanding than first thought and is easily achieved if an effort is made.

When candidates introduce themselves:
- write down their name and their details
- link some visual image to them, for example if one candidate enjoys the theatre, imagine him/her in a period costume
- repeat their name as often and as early as possible.

People need to be recognised and tutors will find this pays dividends very quickly.

Creating Rapport

The key ingredients for creating a rapport with the team of candidates, i.e., the "team", are honesty and respect. The tutor will probably gain respect for the qualifications and experience which led them to the position of becoming a tutor. The key to success is to give confidence to candidates and let them know they can call on this background during the course. However, tutors should also ensure that they never misuse this background by boasting or as a means of intimidation. Candidates will become withdrawn and will reduce their input to the programme. Similarly, since candidates will all have experiences and knowledge to contribute, they should be encouraged to explain and develop these as part of the rapport building exercise.

4.3   Briefing the Team

Regulations and syllabus
Previous references have introduced the notion that tutors should know, understand and apply the NGB regulations. It is also very important that key features of the regulations are explained to the candidates. In effect the regulations form the basis of a "contract" between the tutor and the candidates. They should be able to use them as a means of checking whether or not the tutor is delivering the syllabus. The regulations also ensure that candidates are clear about what is expected of them and how they will be assessed.

Assessment Process
Frequently the course tutor is also the person assessing the candidates. If fair assessments are to be made it is essential that candidates be carefully briefed on the process to be carried out.

- Preparing for assessment of the practical
  Assessment of the practical work, if properly briefed and prepared, should hold no surprises for any candidates. They will still be nervous about it, but at least they will know what is coming to them.

Explain:
- what will be assessed
- that what is being assessed is open to some negotiation, e.g., assessing verbal communication skills for a candidate with a throat infection might need some rearrangement
- when it will happen
- how it will be done
- that an outcome/result will be given
- that an action plan will be provided for their improvement
- that their comments about the process are important
- the role of the Internal Verifier (See also, Part 5, paragraph 5.2, *The Assessment Process – What is involved?*).

Encourage:
- candidates to seek clarification if they are uncertain about what is happening
- candidates to comment on the process they have experienced
- candidates to contribute to their own action planning during the debriefing after the assessment.

Ensure:
- that the candidate is clear about the outcome/result, e.g., *"You are competent in x, y and z areas, but not yet competent in areas d and e"*. NB Comment like, *"You are doing all right"*, is not a clear statement of an outcome
- that the candidate is clear about what has to be done for future development and improvement. This ought to apply to all levels of outcome; even the very able need an action plan (They have paid the same fee as everyone else on the course!), not just the weaker candidates
- that the action plan is as specific as possible, e.g., *"Experiment by standing in a variety of positions to test the use of your voice and check your participants' responses"*, is direct and helpful. *"Improve your voice"*, is less helpful
- the candidate has a clearly written statement of outcome and action plan on the appropriate forms
- that all the appropriate signatures are gained.

- **Assessment of the theory**
  The proper briefing and preparation discussed above in the practical context also apply to the theory work. It should be remembered that theory work often comes as a surprise to inexperienced candidates. A frequent comment is, *"I didn't realise there was so much to it"*.

Generally, candidates are reasonably comfortable about being assessed in the practical context. When it comes to the theory, however, they are often quite frightened, *"I know how to do it, but I cannot write it down"*, and *"I'm no good at exams"*, are frequently made comments. Younger candidates, by definition, are more likely to have had recent assessment experience through school, college or university work, whereas older candidates might be out of touch with the examination process and techniques.

All candidates, however, are still in need of advice about the approach to the assessment. The nature of the questions used, and the answers expected, may well be quite different from their previous experience. For example, the answers expected in the context of sport are likely to be shorter than in other examinations they may have experienced. This may well mean that examination techniques learned in other environments could be counter-productive. The classic method of commencing the answer with a repeat of the part of the question required for many examinations could be inappropriate in the short answer.

As already suggested, the assessment process is based on specific performance criteria derived from the NGB regulations as applied to the course in question. The briefing may well be approached at two levels:

- Firstly, an overview of all the areas to be assessed.

Figure 19 - Example overview

If you refer to pages x – y in your copy of the regulations you will see that you are to be assessed on:
- Your practical teaching/coaching ability
- Your completion of the worksheets and session plans etc in your logbook/portfolio
- Your theoretical knowledge via a written examination lasting …hours
- Your ability to discuss issues and answer questions via verbal questioning

Following the brief overview a more detailed review of each of the areas previously discussed will be needed. It is quite likely that some areas of assessment will need a far more detailed treatment very early on, e.g., the way continuous assessment is carried out, whereas other assessment areas, e.g., the theory examination, might be delayed for a more detailed explanation later during the programme.

- Secondly, a more detailed coverage of selected areas of assessment

Figure 20 - Example detailed coverage

The practical assessment will be made against set performance criteria in:
- your ability to coach
- your ability to carry out accurate and appropriate demonstrations
- your ability to observe accurately and analyse skills
- your ability to provide feedback to individuals and groups of participants
- your ability to work with an assistant
- your ability to maintain a safe environment.

You can find a sample of the assessment form by referring to pages xxx in the regulations. After any assessment you will be given a copy of the completed assessment forms. These will form the basis of discussion, feedback and an action plan pointing up areas upon which you should focus for the next practical session. You will be expected to contribute to the formulation of the action plan through discussion with me and through the use of your self-evaluations.

The actual timing for providing further levels of detail will probably be influenced by the nature and shape of the programme being followed. A course of single weekly sessions spread out over a period of, say, three months, will mean that the detail of the theory examination will not be necessary for many weeks, whilst on a shorter, concentrated course over a week, the examination detail may have to be covered after the third or fourth day.

Theory examination

Not all NGBs use theory examinations as part of the assessment process. However, for those that do use this method it is essential that tutors prepare candidates in the knowledge demanded by the course syllabus. It is equally important that candidates should be prepared for the examination experience itself. Whilst examination questions are probably going to require a greater proportion of "right" answers, even so, there may be times when experience and common sense could prevail.

● **Examination techniques**

There will be matters of concern to the candidates like:

▪ what will the paper look like? Is there a specimen copy?

▪ how much time to allocate to each answer?

▪ what is the possible relationship between the time and the marks on offer per question? (Ten minutes to answer a question offering one mark is not sensible)

▪ common examination advice, e.g., read the question carefully and answer the question as it is set

▪ underline/highlight key words in the question

▪ if the question asks for, say, three examples, causes, reasons etc, only write three not more. Hoping the marker will sort out the best answers is unlikely to work

▪ suggest that the whole paper should be read before attempting any question

▪ if an answer does not come to mind immediately, move on to the next question and return later

▪ if they are shown, look at the number of marks on offer and allocate time accordingly

▪ warn the candidates of their probable first reactions to the paper:

Figure 21 - Example of a candidate's probable first response to a paper

Question 1   *"I can't do it!"*
Question 2   *"Oh dear, I can't do that either!"*
Question 3   The initial panic will begin to subside slightly and a focus on possible answers will begin to develop.

Tutors should encourage candidates to discuss "What ifs...?" to help clear the air of their concerns.

Figure 22 - Example "What ifs?"

Question	*"Can I take spare paper into the exam for rough notes?"*
Answer	"No, make your notes on the spare sheets in the paper and cross them out afterwards so that the marker is not side tracked from the real answer"
Question	*"What happens if I make a mistake?"*
Answer	"Firstly, do not worry. Go to the spare sheets in the paper, write the question number and part (Do no write out the question itself) and then the answer. Then go back and cross out the first answer. Do this last just in case you run out of time or you change your mind and decide to leave it"
Question	*"Is it better to leave blank spaces rather than write a wrong answer?"*
Answer	"Usually, no. Remember, if you write nothing you will have no chance of gaining a mark. Something written might mean some credit might be given"

The whole issue of assessment is of considerable importance. Accurate assessment is not easy and tutors/assessors should constantly remind themselves of the need to arrive at fair assessment outcomes. Remember, prospective jobs may be riding on the back of the outcome of the course. Further assessment matters are developed in Part 5, *Assessment Decisions*.

4.4   Delivering the Theory

Introduction
The issues of methodology, planning, timing and preparing have already been covered in Parts 1-3 of the book. However, it would be useful to review the key issues.

Summary of decisions to be made prior to delivery:
- What are the objectives of session?
- What is the priority?
- What methodology will help in the achievement of the outcomes?
- How will achievement be identified? What measures will be used?
- How can the candidates be involved (Questions/answers, tasks, activities)?

- If the candidates are involved how much time will it take for the task itself and a review?
- Does this need the help/input of other candidates?
- Is the environment conducive to learning? Examples:
  - are external distractions minimised to ensure full concentration?
  - is there provision for a range of AVAs to add variety?
  - do the rooms have adequate heating, lighting, and ventilation?
  - how comfortable/suitable is the seating that is available?
  - how good are the acoustics?
  - are there any power points, where are they situated? Will an extension lead be needed?
  - is it possible to darken the room easily?

The best way to check that all the facilities are available, or can be obtained, is to inspect the accommodation in advance (*"Case the joint"!*). If possible, be there at least one hour before the start to give time to correct any failures.

Check out the candidates - To communicate effectively, the tutor must gear the sessions to the candidates being addressed. Before delivering the material consider the group needs. These could be identified at the introduction. At the planning stage the minimum level of knowledge was assumed. This might not be the case when the candidates meet for the first time!

Remember, before the start, the method used by presenters of the news on television. *"Tell them what you are going to tell them, tell them, and then tell them what you have told them"*. In other words give an outline of the subject using main headings, deliver the detail, and finally summarise what has been covered. This is a tried and trusted method for assisting memory recall.

A useful mnemonic to remember at the start is **INTRO**
- **I**nterest   – raise the candidates' interest in the subject in some way.
- **N**eed   – tell them what's in it for them and why they should listen.
- **T**ime   – tell them how long the session will take and stick to it!
- **R**ange   – tell then what the will session cover.
- **O**utcomes   – tell them the objectives of the session.

Objectives and Outcomes - Start any formal delivery by explaining the outcomes of the session in terms they will understand. For example, candidates at the end of this session will know:

- the principles of teaching/coaching
- the contents of an EAP or NOP
- the outline structure of a lesson/session plan.

Maintain the candidates' attention and concentration by ensuring that they understand the relevance and importance of the content. They must know what is in it for them if they are going to listen.

As suggested in Part 1, paragraph 1.5, *Creating a Learning Evironment*, since the level of interaction with candidates tends to be low, the lecture method is only appropriate as a means of transferring knowledge. However, short, informative lectures are extremely important and should precede any group work that relies on the application of knowledge to form competence. Having introduced the session the tutor should proceed to deliver information following a clear structure and, where possible, using a variety of visual aids.

Positioning - Inexperienced tutors may be feeling nervous when first getting up to speak, so positioning is important. Try to feel comfortable and stand where it is most appropriate for the situation. The main advantage of standing up is that everyone can see the tutor, but it may also be a more convenient position from which to manipulate any visual materials. Additionally the tutor may feel more "in charge". Try to avoid becoming fixed to one spot or, conversely, pace the floor like a caged animal. With a small group seated around a conference table the informality level will be high and it is probably more appropriate for the tutor to sit, too. The greater the level of informality, the more vulnerable the tutor can become and inexperienced tutors should consider this point during their first courses. Standing behind a table with the group out in front might create a barrier between the tutor and the candidates, but it might also be a comfort to someone early on in their tutoring career.

Establish eye contact - A sea of faces at the beginning can be very off putting and most tutors tend to fear making mistakes in front of others. Even the most experienced tutors suffer feelings of inadequacy or stage fright at times. This sensitivity is simply a timely reminder of our own fallibility and limitations and can be our strongest asset in helping overcome the first few minutes of a lecture.

Some suggestions for dealing with those early experiences are:
- on rising to start, allow 5-10 seconds before beginning to speak. Breathe deeply (but quietly) collect a few final thoughts then begin. This momentary pause will also give the candidates time to settle
- memorise the first sentence or so of the introduction
- look around, pick an interested or friendly face and start by directing the talk to that person, then quickly look for another then another
- cultivate the candidates – seek "acceptability"
- speak to all the candidates, not just one or two. Remember those out of sight on the ends!
- don't fix a gaze at one particular person for too long.

Delivery style - It is important that tutors convey their own knowledge, experience and humour using anecdotes, where appropriate, to bring the subject to life. There is nothing more mind numbing than pure theory without living examples to explain it. At the same time, the approach must be relevant to the outcomes and the needs and interests of the candidates. Use a personal style of presenting and be aware that the candidates are still largely unknown quantities:

- Be careful in the choice of language or humour. A thoughtless word or gesture may create barriers to communication that will be difficult to overcome later.
- Be natural. Don't try to imitate anyone else.
- Be enthusiastic and sincere in what is said and done. It can be infectious.

All actions and gestures should be purposeful, natural, and designed to emphasise a particular point. If presentations are rehearsed check for any mannerisms that might distract the candidates.

The most common mannerisms to avoid include:
- jingling coins, playing with chalk, pen or pointer
- flapping hands or waving arms, adjusting ties, notes, spectacles
- excessive *"Ums"* and *"Errs"*, or repeated use of particular words or phrases (e.g., *"You know"*, *"OK"*, or *"Do you know what I mean?"*)
- constant tapping of the table top whilst speaking.

Some tutors become so concerned about mannerisms that they work hard to eradicate them altogether. However, depending on the original problem, this can sometimes result in a robot-like delivery lacking in any natural speech or movement. The answer is to be aware of gestures and mannerisms and know which ones are potential distractions and work to keep them under control.

Making the most of the voice - Effective use of the voice is essential if the candidates' regard for the tutor is to be maintained, and if they are to retain their interest in what is being said. Some people, when they are in front of a group, tend to lose some of their expressiveness. Having a rehearsal might help to aid memory recall and allow the tutor to focus on delivery rather than content. The main areas to consider are:

- **Pacing the delivery** - Tutors are inclined to race their initial presentations, which lead to loss of clarity through gabbling. A funeral pace not only bores people but also allows them to jump ahead. If the problem is racing, take more breaths between sentences, and cultivate pauses. Vary the pace, slow the tempo to emphasise important points, and quicken it for lighter moments. Pauses can also be very good for effect - they create suspense and allow an idea to sink in. Rushing on without a pause means that important points may be lost. If humour is used don't talk over the laughter, assuming there is any!

- **The tone of voice** - Try to vary the tone of voice to convey confidence, emotion, emphasis etc. Altering the volume also provides variety and reduces the chances of monotony. Make sure nerves don't affect audibility. For example, it is very easy to inadvertently allow the voice to tail off at the end of sentences. Speak out to the candidates, and throw the voice to the back row so that all can hear. This does not mean that shouting has to be used. Trying to stretch the vocal chords beyond their designed limits is futile and may leave the speaker hoarse or speechless. If the pitch of the voice is likely to present problems then perhaps consider the use of a microphone. This will make voice projection simpler and will save the added worries of vocal acrobatics!

- **Use language suited to the audience** - Whilst candidates may be able to hear what is said, they may not understand it.
  Guarding against this means:
  - avoiding the use of words that are outside the realm of the candidates' knowledge and experience. If this is necessary, because of the nature of the information, explain the meanings and use of the words or phrases
  - avoiding the excessive use of abbreviations. If they must be used for brevity's sake, make sure that they are familiar with them or, if not, explain first what they mean
  - avoiding the use of slang or words that may be easily misunderstood
  - avoiding the use of emotive words, unless the intension is to agitate or excite feelings
  - being careful when contemplating telling funny stories. Make sure they work by trying them out on other unfortunate people!

Lecture and Lesson Methods

Previous references, Part 1, paragraph 1.5, *Creating a Learning Environment,* and Part 3, paragraph 3.7, *Preparing the Session Notes,* have covered the lesson method in some detail. The key difference between a lecture and a lesson is the level of participation the candidates have within the session. If the application of knowledge is essential to candidate learning then the lecture becomes less productive and the lesson becomes a better option. In these cases, the tutor will need to use exercises that allow the candidates to experience the application of the new information, or share their experiences and personal knowledge with others, to bring relevance to the subject. Simple exercises can be dealt with in the classroom with candidates working in pairs, threes or alone, but for larger, more complex exercises, group working in separate areas or rooms might be needed.

Clearly, if time is to be given to candidates to apply knowledge, the lesson will take much longer than the lecture, and the tutor will need to switch roles during group work and become a facilitator.

The process of delivering a lesson might be:
- start the lesson using the same methodology as a lecture
- provide the necessary technical input in the form of a short lecture
- brief the candidates on the exercise explaining the exact requirements

- divide the candidates into pairs, threes or groups of four to six
- specify timescales and report back details
- facilitate the group work (See paragraph 4.7)
- review outcomes in plenary (See Part 8, *Glossary*) and identify key learning points
- summarise the session and thank candidates for their work.

It could also be useful to remind the groups that they are unlikely to have sufficient time to complete the task to their satisfaction but, nevertheless, they will begin to understand the nature of the problem set, and its resolution, as a result of doing the task.

Figure 23 – Example of Group work

In groups of 4

You have 10 minutes to carry out the following task.

- Brainstorm   *"What makes an effective teacher/coach"*
- Structure the output by separating the ideas into qualities and skills
- One person from each group to present the findings in plenary (3 minutes).

Good luck!

The time taken for the lesson will be made up of the tutor's technical input, the time duration of the task, the feedback (3 minutes x 4), and the time taken for the review and summary. As previously emphasised, although there are time penalties for candidate participation, if used appropriately, learning will be greatly enhanced.

Discussion Method

This method encourages candidates to call upon their experience and knowledge and where opinions are put to the test. The level of tutor input, ideally, is very low as the tutor role moves more towards facilitation, whilst the candidates' input will be very high. This calls for skilful use of the tutor's leadership skills to ensure that all candidates are given the opportunity to speak and that strong individuals are not allowed to dominate the debate. This method can be used with the whole group or in smaller sub-groups. With the latter the leadership and facilitation roles will have to be delegated, therefore great care should be taken to control their progress. The method can form a complete session or can be embedded within a lesson.

Whatever the method:
- agree the ground rules for the discussion group(s)
- appoint roles, e.g., chairman, facilitator, observer, "note taker", and timekeeper etc
- define clearly the objective and expected outcomes
- set timescales for the debate
- follow the discussion with a summary of the key issues raised.

Figure 24 - Example use of discussion

Group: All candidates
Timescale: 15 minutes
Subject: Dealing with the difficult parent
Objective: At the end of the session the group will have agreed, using consensus reaching, a checklist reminder that candidates can use to deal with difficult parents.
Chairman:
Facilitator:
Observer:
Note taker:
Timekeeper:

When the discussion is underway the tutor should allow the debate to flow, observing the process being used, and ensure that the topic and objectives are being followed. Tutor intervention might be necessary if the group deviates from the task, or if one person begins to dominate. A suggestion such as, *"Can we just revisit the objectives for a minute?"* will resolve the situation. A reminder of ground rules and an observation of what is going on in terms of process will usually help get the group back on track. Prior "contracting" with the team is important if conflict is to be avoided. If the group is expecting tutor intervention it will not be surprised when it happens.

Role-Play Method
Where it is important for a candidate to practise skills involving interaction with others role-play is the ideal method to cover the theory. Although it is 'stage managed' it can be very close to reality, and it does allow candidates to experience the skills needed. It is surprising that, when a candidate is asked to act in a specific role, e.g., an angry sports centre manager, how real it becomes.

Indeed, tutors with little experience of role-play activities should be warned that great care and sensitivity will be required. Sometimes the "play" is forgotten, and the role character takes over. This can produce serious tension within the group. The method can be used in plenary with the whole group or in smaller sub-groups, depending on the exercise chosen. This will determine how long is needed.

The process:
- Brief the candidates on the role-play exercise.
- Allocate who plays what role and observer(s).
- Set ground rules.
- Set timescales (Allow for all candidates taking the roles).
- Run the exercises.
- Review outcomes and summarise key learning points.

It is important that each candidate gets the opportunity to practise the key role, e.g., *'The teacher/coach dealing with a difficult child'*, and that the other roles are played as realistically as possible. The success of the session will be enhanced if there is a clear set of ground rules and the roles are well defined.

Figure 25 – Example of role-play exercise

Subject: Talking to a group of parents.
Objective: To allow candidates to role-play a teacher/coach giving a
            5-minute talk to a group of parents on the subject of nutrition.
Groups: Three groups of four candidates.

Careful time management skills will be needed to control the activities and, as can be seen above, for all four candidates in each group to experience the role it will take at least 20 minutes. The tutor needs to make sure that individuals do not monopolise the time and deprive others of their turn.

Case Studies

These are scenarios a teacher/coach may need to deal with in terms of problem solving or decision-making. They can be used in a variety of contexts and serve as a vehicle from which theory can be discussed.

Figure 26 - Example of case study

Syllabus: Athlete/Swimmer motivation

Susan is a nervous child who attends your session each Monday morning at
9.00 am. Just lately she has been missing sessions and when she does arrive
she seems to isolate herself from other children. Once the session starts she
is very receptive, listens and tries hard to achieve the goals given, but when
the session is over she rushes off quickly without staying to talk to anyone
in the group.

How would you deal with the situation?

When using case studies time must be allowed for candidates to read the
material and raise questions before they begin to work on them.

4.5   Delivering the Practical

Working with candidates
The ability to work with candidates, facilitate their learning and give specific,
positive feedback so that they are able to develop new competencies are
essential features of the tutor role. At times, general feedback on aspects
common to all candidates can be useful in raising awareness. However, it is
important that the tutor does not deprive the candidates of the opportunity to
learn by offering to help too much, too soon. It must be remembered that the
primary reason for running the course is for the candidates' benefit, so priority
must be given to addressing candidate needs. The needs of tutor and
participants are of secondary importance unless, of course, a matter of safety is
involved.

The tutor needs to establish a practical environment which:
• gives each candidate practice in all relevant areas of the syllabus
• allows for observations and analysis of candidate performance.

The tutor will need to establish an environment that allows candidates to perform in a variety of contexts:
- by giving specific feedback to candidates during and after practical
- by confirming final *competent/not yet competent* outcomes to candidate
- by helping candidates with their development action plans.

Working with participants
To give candidates the opportunity to develop their practical teaching/coaching skills NGB programmes often make use of participants who role-play athletes, swimmers, opposing teams etc., in a formal situation. These participants are an extremely valuable resource since they offer opportunities of creating a wide variety of conditions approximating to those met in the workplace. It is important that the tutor acts as the leader and performs all the leadership tasks associated with this group in order to gain their confidence and support. It is also important to stress to the participants and, if relevant, their parents, both that the candidate teacher/coaches are not yet fully qualified and the purpose of the course.

It will greatly help if the tutor:
- explains the purpose of the course
- gains their support for the candidates and course
- explains all the relationships, e.g., candidates to participants
- explains the rotation and changes that will effect them
- recognises and acknowledges the contribution (If the participants are young children, some tutors reward them with sweets at the end of the course!).

The tutor will need to demonstrate a variety of practical exercises to give candidates a view of the task they are tackling. This might entail the tutor working with the participants whilst providing the candidates with an explanation. This is often referred to as 'the learning triangle', and tutors need to develop this key competence.

Figure 27 - The learning triangle

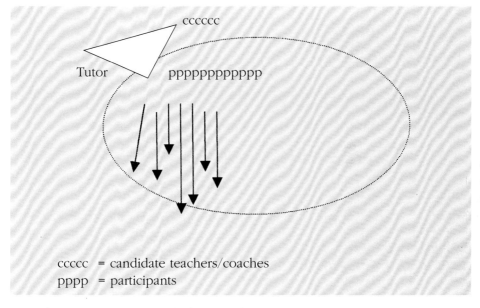

ccccc = candidate teachers/coaches
pppp = participants

Two dangers associated with the triangle are:
● the tutor gives a lecture/lesson to candidates to the exclusion of participants
● the tutor teaches/coaches participants to the exclusion of candidates.

It is important that the tutor shows the candidates how to demonstrate key skills whilst managing and communicating with participants, at the same time explaining clearly to candidates the reasons why decisions and actions have been taken. The maintenance of the triangle to facilitate observation and communication is a key issue.

Carrying out assessments
The tutor will need to observe, assess, and give feedback to each of the candidates throughout the course. Early feedback is essential if candidates are to be given time to improve their performance, and time must be allocated for this confidential information. The tutor will also need time to give *competent/not yet competent* outcomes both during and at the conclusion of the course. Additionally, time will be needed not only to assess candidate

logbook/portfolios, exercises and other tasks which will influence overall performance, but also to the provision of feedback on these areas. It is, therefore, essential to allocate time for each of these activities in the tutor's personal time plan that supplements the course timetable. In Part 2, paragraph 2.11, *Further Factors in the Design and Organisation of a Course,* there was a task, *Planning for assessment,* to assist in the considerations of the implications of this key activity in the practical context.

4.6   The Testing of Understanding

A sound education programme is not about absorbing information and facts simply "to pass" the examination. In fact, education does not really take place until there is evidence of understanding and the ability to apply the learning to a variety of contexts. Testing candidate understanding, therefore, is of considerable importance.

Preparing for assessment of the theory

- Worksheets - Often candidates approach worksheets with a lack of confidence. They need to be encouraged to use their own initiative, and to understand that not all questions have right/wrong answers. Many questions may demand the application of candidates' previous, personal experience and old-fashioned common sense. They are frightened of getting an answer "wrong" when, in fact, there is probably no one right, or wrong, answer. The real issue is, *"What do you* (The candidate) *think you would do here?"* or, *"What do you think should happen here?"* and so on.

- Feedback - A major part of the role of the tutor is the provision of feedback. Candidates have a right to it. The marking of worksheet material is no exception and this means more than simply ticking answers. In the same way that feedback in the practical context is usually a mixture of praise and confirmation, e.g., *"Well done, your use of the space has greatly improved",* so, too, in the theory context we might need something like, *"Your hard work on the physiology material seems to be paying off."* Similarly, encouragement to pursue an answer just a little further might come in the form a short written comment in the margin, e.g., *"Can you find two further points about this?"*

If tutor comments are likely to be extensive, it is probably better that they are made on separate sheets of paper. This method is particularly true of comments and feedback on session plans where space is limited, and when participants might see the material during the ensuing practical session. Excessive remarks/scribbles over the face of candidates' work can be a reminder of the treatment they might have received at school and belittle their efforts. Nobody should lose his or her dignity during the assessment process, no matter whether it is in the practical or the theory situation. (See also Part 5, paragraph 5.3, *The Assessment – How is it done?*

Preparation techniques for candidates

- Homework – This is probably, the most often used technique for preparing candidates for the theory examination, often through the use of specimen questions set during the course. There are other techniques which might be explored. The classic method mentioned above undoubtedly produces good results for hardworking candidates. However, as in life in general, there is a downside:
  - It does not develop appropriate examination short answering techniques.
  - Candidates often simply copy from books.
  - Candidates often spend excessive amounts of time and writing large amounts of material to answer the questions.
  - More tutor time is taken up in marking overlong answers.
  - It may not help the tutor identify real weaknesses in the candidates' knowledge and understanding.
  - It places excessive burdens on the candidate time when, perhaps, they should be preparing material for future practical sessions and reading the books which support the programme.

- Short tests - These are set as questions and written in the style of examination questions. The time allocated for the answering should approximate to the amount of time a candidate would get in an examination, say, two or three minutes per answer. Such a test might consist of perhaps three or four questions at the beginning of each theory session. Occasionally, usually towards the middle of the course, a slightly longer test might be set with eight to ten questions. The questions could be based on the reading set for that session, or all work done previously, or a mixture of both.

This approach provides:
- the candidate with good examination paper experience in realistic time
- both the candidate and tutor with a good reflection of candidates' performance under pressure
- both the candidate and tutor with a better chance of using precious time more productively.

- **The mock examination** - This technique is frequently used and can take an hour or more. This is not necessarily a disadvantage, simply a reminder of the time needed, in the same way that short tests referred to above could take, five/ten minutes every session for the whole course. It clearly gives both candidates an excellent "feel" for examination conditions. However, if it is carried out during the penultimate session of the course before the examination proper is taken, it gives very little time for both tutor and candidate to make use of the outcomes as the basis of feedback for the real thing. Unless candidates receive feedback on their performance the value of the experience is very limited.

- **Marking of work in general** - Tutors should try to mark work as soon as possible after they receive it. The most common practice is to receive work at the end of one session and return next session. This clearly works, although the time delay means that any feedback received is too late to implement next time. This could have a serious effect on a weaker candidate who might argue that if the feedback had been provided earlier things could have been improved. This issue is developed in Part 7, paragraph 7.4, *Postal Work and Distance Learning.*

- **Revision techniques** - Good revision needs to be planned. For many candidates the examination might be the first they have sat since leaving school. If candidates have their own revision techniques which have worked before, and with which they feel comfortable - encourage them to use them. Other candidates might need help:
  - Encourage them to create a revision timetable spanning a period of time leading up to the examination. Revising for the first time the day/night before the examination is not a good idea. It is more of a panic measure and will not be very productive.

- Having created a revision timetable, encourage the candidates to keep to it. If it has been well thought through it should take care of most, if not all, key issues.
- Recognise that, in the real world, candidates have pressures, both workplace and domestic. Their revision should reflect this. Frequent shorter periods, extending over 20 or 30 minutes, are more likely to be achievable than trying to set aside "*The whole of Sunday*". The short periods have a greater chance of being totally focused, e.g., telephones ringing, canaries dying, etc, can become someone else's problem during that time.

Encourage candidates to discuss their revision programme with each other. They can be mutually supportive, often by creating revision groups, either by meeting as such or by telephoning each other.

4.7   Facilitating Groups and Individuals

Moving from formal lecturing to a method that allows candidates to gain competence through 'doing' means that interactive tutoring becomes more important to develop effective learning. The tutor will gradually move into a possibly more demanding role of a facilitator. As candidate participation is so important, and as a large percentage of the tutor's time will be spent working with groups and individuals, the need for effective facilitation becomes a key competence. This role is best described as being similar to that of the golfer's caddie. It is the golfer who plays the shots and learns from experience, not the caddie. It is the golfer that makes the decisions and solves problems along the way. The caddie, however, is essential to the learning process and is a source of feedback acting as a sounding board for the golfer, and only giving personal advice when it is actively sought. The caddie will also challenge and force the golfer into clear thinking. The relationship may go through difficult periods when they cannot agree but the golfer knows the value of this aspect of the caddie's role and has respect for it. As suggested earlier, when setting tasks be careful not to deprive the candidate of the opportunity to learn through the solving of problems and making decisions. Let them struggle with the new skills before stepping in.

Additional competencies demanded by the facilitation role

Technical Competence means:
- understanding the learning process and associated learning styles
- understanding candidates and how they behave in formal situations
- understanding group dynamics.

Contracting Skills means:
- gaining agreements on their role with individuals and groups
- building rapport and trust with individuals and groups.

Interpersonal Skills means:
- being assertive
- being able to clarify and summarise
- being able to give non-judgmental feedback on performance
- being able to address candidates' fears.

Process Skills means:
- understanding the difference between process and content
- establishing a supportive environment
- supporting learning from experiences
- confronting difficult issues
- knowing when to intervene and when to withdraw.

Observation and Analysis means:
- carrying out behavioural analysis of groups and individuals
- analysing body language and non-verbal signals
- identifying when individuals and groups need help.

Facilitating the Individual

All candidates will have differing needs in relation to facilitation. Generally they will require feedback in various ways and it is important that the tutor recognises this. The observation and analysis of performance relating to course syllabus requirements is non-negotiable and there are the mandatory aspects of written feedback and assignments that cannot be changed. However, in other areas such as behaviours and styles, candidates may require personal input from the tutor. In these situations the tutor should ensure that the candidates' needs are met and that feedback given in an agreed format, thereby avoiding any hurt feelings. Some individuals may prefer written comments, whilst others may prefer face-to-face verbal feedback.

When giving feedback the tutor should ensure that:
- candidates' self- esteem is maintained at all times
- feedback is objective and non-judgemental
- feedback methods are agreed with the candidate.

Facilitating Groups

There will be a number of occasions on a course where group work is necessary to allow skill practice. In these situations facilitation becomes very important to ensure that all candidates gain from the experience. At the beginning of the course the role should be explained and agreement from the candidates sought so that there are no misunderstandings of what is likely to happen. Having contracted in this way from day one there will be little need to raise the matter, other than a reminder when each group session begins.

Setting group tasks entails:
- providing the necessary technical input needed for the candidates (lecture or lesson)
- testing that the technical knowledge is understood by all candidates
- briefing the group on the task (sheets with the task detailed are helpful)
- agreeing timescales and reporting back requirements, e.g., presentation, discussion methods
- allowing the group to work through the task
- facilitating the group until the task is complete
- recording and summarising key learning points.

Having given all candidates the technical input needed to perform the task, e.g., write a one hour, early season session plan for a group of senior athletes or swimmers, their basic understanding should be checked. Be careful to clearly brief the task, timescales and method of reporting back and, if possible, have this written down with the objectives. It is very important to allow the groups to establish themselves and begin working before the tutor becomes involved. This period will often be used by the candidates to clarify the task given. Once they have started, after a short period, say 5 minutes, the tutor should start visiting the groups to ask if the task is clear. They will be expecting both the visit and the questions because they will have contracted with the tutor on day one. Sometimes they might not fully understand the task set or, perhaps, misunderstand the requirements of the task. If this is the case the tutor should clarify the requirement and withdraw from the group.

After they have worked on the task for a period of time the tutor should re-visit the groups and check to see how they are proceeding. If they are on the right track they can be left to carry on, if not then some help should be offered, but without doing the task for them. A simple statement such as *'I heard Jane make a suggestion a few moments ago but I am not sure you all heard it'*, may resolve the roadblock. The tutor should try to avoid giving the solution and, when visiting groups, be prepared to be assertive and get them to stick to the ground rules, thus ensuring that they follow a structured process and that all candidates are involved. Questions such as, *'Why are you discussing youngsters when the task is for seniors?'* are much more powerful in re-focussing the group on the task than critical comments like *'I told you the exercise was for seniors?"* This might alienate them and take their minds off the task.

When the task is completed, or the time allocated has elapsed, prompt the groups to return to plenary and present the findings. Finally, test understanding when the groups present their work and raise questions to provoke debate. Tutors, by involving themselves in the presentations, may be helping to identify gaps in knowledge and will be making a valuable contribution to the candidates' understanding. Feedback to groups follows the same criteria as individuals. They should be congratulated on their hard work, be dealt with sensitively when they present material that is inaccurate, but make sure that explanation is offered on why it was wrong. Tutors should recognise all that is correct and reinforce the key points.

Part 5

Assessment Decisions

5.1 Introduction to Assessment

A number of assessment issues have already been discussed in previous sections of the book (See Part 2, paragraph 2.11, *Further Factors in the Design and Organisation of a Course*, Part 4, paragraph 4.3, *Briefing the Team* and 4.5, *Delivering the Practical*), whilst other aspects of preparing for the assessment process are touched upon in Part 4, paragraph 4.6, *The Testing of Understanding*).

Normally, candidate teachers/coaches do not enter the assessment process on the basis that it will be easy. By presenting themselves for assessment they are demonstrating that they wish to attain a given standard, preferably a national standard. This is of particular importance in the current climate of flexibility in the employment market. Accurate assessment is the key to maintaining these standards. With the advent of National Vocational Qualifications (NVQs) in 1986, and their subsequent adoption in sport and recreation, there entered a sharper focus in the assessment process. No matter whether or not the assessments are in relation to the National Standards, as defined by the Qualifications and Curriculum Authority (QCA), the body which now oversees the standards, the method of assessment will probably reflect the influence of NVQs and the QCA in some way.

In many NGBs tutors are both tutors and assessors. For the purposes of this discussion they are going to be referred to as "tutor/assessors".

Tutor/assessors can sometimes forget what it is like to be assessed as candidates lower down the pecking order. It is important that they help prepare their candidates so that they are familiar with the process through which they will be going.

5.2 The Assessment Process - What is involved?

Methods of assessment

It is usual for the assessment process to be more than one final "death or glory" judgement. The most common methods of assessment are "continuous" and "final":

- **Continuous assessment**
  As the name implies, it is ongoing and, therefore, occurs on more than one occasion. Properly used it forms a valuable part of the candidates' learning process because:
  - it informs them about their current performance
  - it identifies strengths
  - it identifies areas for development and the additional support required to improve
  - it helps both candidate and tutor/assessor in arriving at an appropriate action plan.

NGB regulations may state the minimum number of assessment opportunities each candidate should have during the training programme. All candidates, no matter what their ability, must have at least the minimum number of assessments stated. These assessments are carried out using whatever the assessment tools and checklists are currently in use. Continuous assessments are, by implication, snapshots of a candidate at a given time during the training programme. These snapshots will not necessarily be of the candidate as a whole. Probably they will be of areas covered during the training programme so far, and on which a tutor/assessor can reasonably expect that the candidate will have a basic understanding.

Continuous assessment can present some rather difficult dilemmas. One example might be that during an early phase of the training programme a candidate's first assessment identifies a serious weakness which simply cannot be ignored. It might be argued that, because it so near the beginning of the course, the candidate really has not had time to grasp the points adequately, so the tutor/assessor might feel that some gentle encouragement is all that is really needed, rather than the rather more formal approach of the assessment process. However, it is essential that the candidate's performance be recorded in such a way that both candidate and tutor/assessor can make reference to it on a future occasion, e.g., in writing and against the standards.

- **Final Assessment** - This should not be construed as the day of judgement; it is simply the last of the continuous assessment opportunities. It should provide the candidate with an outcome of either *"Competent"* or *"Not yet competent"*, and will be based on evidence generated during the continuous assessment process. Normally, if the continuous assessments have been carried out properly, the final outcome should present few, if any, surprises to either the candidate or the tutor/assessor.

- **The responsibilities of those involved in the assessment process**

The candidate - The candidate's responsibility is to work towards the achievement of the current standards as set. Part of that responsibility is to take ownership of their own learning needs and development, i.e., to be constantly trying to figure out their own strengths and areas for development, and looking for ways to enhance the former and address the latter. They should not simply be waiting to be told what they have or have not done and what they will have to do in order to improve.

The tutor/assessor - The tutor/assessors' responsibilities are to ensure:
- that the standards set are maintained
- that the candidates are assessed against the current standards
- that the evidence offered by the candidates is consistent with the NGB demands, e.g., assessment on more than one occasion
- that the evidence offered by the candidates is current/recent/up to date
- that the evidence offered by the candidates is sufficient for decisions/outcomes to be reached
- that the candidates are involved in their own assessment by encouraging them to contribute to it
- that the candidates are provided with feedback
- that the candidate is provided with an action plan. The candidate should have contributed to that plan, i.e., it has been negotiated with the candidate
- that the candidates are aware of their levels of performance, i.e., that they are *"competent"* or *"not yet competent"*, or whatever other method the NGB uses for recording an assessment outcome.

The Internal Verifier - The Internal Verifier (IV) will have considerable experience in assessing and carries serious responsibilities in the assessment process. If the NGB qualifications are aligned to NVQs, the IV is the link between the candidate and the Approved (Assessment) Centre, e.g., the National Governing Body.

The responsibilities include:
- the monitoring of the assessment process and the use of the national standards
- the provision of support for a group of tutor/assessors
- the sampling of the work done by the tutor/assessors. The amount of the

sampling is usually expressed in percentage terms, but will often be determined by a number of factors, e.g., the experience of the tutor/assessor and the familiarity of the IV with individual tutor/assessor's previous use of the standards. In some NGBs the sampling process for some aspects of the work is 100%

- the assessment of evidence provided to the assessor by candidate teacher/coaches, observed, written or spoken, to try to confirm candidate competency or not
- the provision of feedback to tutor/assessors
- liaison with the Approved (Assessment) Centre/NGB and the appointed External Verifier (See below) whenever it is appropriate to do so
- Encouraging assessors to make the initial assessment decisions which then become subject to sampling process, i.e, the Internal Verifiers' role is not about making difficult assessment decisions on behalf of the assessor.

For economic efficiency reasons some NGBs may assign additional duties to the IV to cover a wider variety of administrative tasks and checks to be undertaken during the visits. These additional tasks may well not be part of the IV role as described above (and expanded upon later) but, nevertheless, they will be important, integral aspects of the NGBs monitoring their teacher/coach education programmes.

The External Verifier - The External Verifier (EV) is appointed by the Awarding Body, e.g., City and Guilds, and is external to the Approved (Assessment) Centre. Again, this only applies if the NGB has aligned its qualification to NVQs.

The role of the EV is:
- to verify that the Approved (Assessment) Centre's performance in ensuring quality and consistency against the national standards is appropriate
- to support and advise the Approved (Assessment) Centre in its development.

The EV also operates on a sampling basis. Since the External Verifier often carries a remit for a whole National Governing Body s/he is highly unlikely to be seen as frequently as an Internal Verifier.

It should not be forgotten, however, that the EV is appointed by an Awarding Body to monitor, on behalf of that body, the quality of the delivery of the national standards. A key feature of an EV's responsibilities is to submit reports to the Awarding Body on the outcomes of visits and make recommendations about future actions to be taken. The EV has power to either recommend suspension or withdrawal of an Approved (Assessment) Centre's status to deliver programmes against the national standards should it be appropriate.

Some candidates and, indeed, some tutor/assessors, look upon "assessment" with both dread and as a necessary evil. However, this approach fails to address some important issues:

- The status of the standards, both within the sport and in the eyes of potential "employers", no matter whether they be working as a volunteer or being paid for their work, is built upon the knowledge that those who qualify provide a quality, technically up to date and professional service.
- A properly applied assessment process is a valuable and powerful means of helping candidates improve.
- Assessment and feedback/support for candidates are not incompatible, they are complementary when the assessment process is correctly used.
- Until the candidate is formally measured against the appropriate standards, their strengths and weaknesses, better defined as *areas for development*, cannot be clearly identified relative to those standards and, consequently, the appropriate action plans cannot be negotiated with them.

Where a NGB has aligned its standards to NVQs it means the standards of that NGB are related to national standards across industry in general and, consequently, an even greater measure of quality is encouraged.

5.3 The Assessment - How is it done?

Assessment is based on evidence.
The sources of that evidence could be:
- an observation of the candidate's performance. This is the most powerful form of evidence
- questioning the candidate in a variety of methods
- reports/projects supplied by the candidate

- witness testimonies from a variety of sources (See Part 8, *Glossary)*
- products or materials generated as a result of the candidate's performance.

Evidence to be used by the assessor should be considered against the following:
- Is the evidence valid? (Relevant to what is being assessed)
- Is the evidence authentic? (Produced by the candidate – sometimes making use of witness testimony (See Part 8, *Glossary)*
- Is the evidence current? (Recent and up to date)
- Is the evidence sufficient? (Enough evidence upon which to make assessment decisions)
- Is the evidence consistent? (Can be performed on more than one occasion in normal workplace conditions).

Assessment of the practical
By their very nature, the arrangements for the assessment of practical teaching/coaching require very careful planning in terms of:
- what is to be assessed
- the criteria against which the assessment is to be made
- the availability of the appropriate paperwork
- the candidate briefing/discussion
- the candidate debriefing for feedback, action planning and a statement of outcomes
- the overall allocation of time for the assessment.

Ideally, like most feedback, the debriefing should be carried out immediately after the candidate has finished the assessment session in question. Whilst this may not always be possible, every effort should be made for the debriefing to occur as soon as possible after the event. (For further reference to time allocation for the practical assessment see Part 2, paragraph 2.11, *Further Factors in the Design and Organisation of a Course*, Task 3 – *Planning for Assessment).*

The assessment of the practical has further implications related to the tutor/assessor's observation position, e.g., close enough to hear and see what is being said and done, but far enough away to avoid overwhelming the candidate. In order to overcome this dilemma most assessors often change their observation position according to the changing context of the session being observed. One other essential matter to be taken into account by the tutor/assessor is that, whilst the individual assessments are being carried, out a careful watch on the rest of the candidates and participants must be maintained, even if only to ensure that the environment remains safe.

Supporting candidates in the theory work

It is important that tutor/assessors make sure that:

- they help and encourage candidates organise their time. Remember, for many of them this might be the first time since leaving school that they have undertaken any formal study. One way of helping them is to set deadlines and schedules for completing work. The earlier they know these the better, preferably before the programme commences
- the candidates understand their responsibilities to note the above deadlines and make every effort to complete the work accordingly. Failure to make deadlines will mean that the candidate suffers the additional stress of trying to catch up
- the candidates understand that, if a problem of workload arises, they should consult the tutor/assessor as soon as possible.

Tutor/assessors should also remember that, if a candidate falls behind with work, and requires additional attention, the remainder of the group should not get less attention.

The marking of written work:

Marking written work is seldom an exciting experience, but it goes with the territory!

Tutors/assessors should ensure that:

- they have made provision for sufficient time for all work created by candidates to receive a full treatment
- all candidates' work is treated with respect by the tutor/assessor. Most candidates put a great deal of time and effort into their work. It deserves to be treated accordingly
- only very brief comments are written on the actual work, e.g., writing all over the work is very insensitive and can demotivate the candidate
- most comments are written on either the reverse side of their sheet, if blank, or on a separate sheet of paper using a cross-referencing system, e.g., a "1" in the margin corresponds to a "note 1" on the separate sheet

- some form of brief vocabulary is created which clearly indicates what has to be done, e.g., *"Resubmit Q2a"*; *"I think we should discuss this"*; *"What other activities could you have used?"* *"See note..."*; *"You appear to have understood the general principles of session planning"*
- all work receives some form of feedback on what has been achieved. This might be specific to a question, or more general, and sums up the candidate's understanding or lack of it, or the progress being made.

Providing feedback and action planning - check that:
- the feedback is brief and focuses on key issues. There may be five areas to be addressed but, probably, say, three are more important than the rest
- the feedback is provided as soon as possible after the candidate has been observed
- the candidate understands the feedback and is encouraged to discuss it
- the feedback is based on fact, i.e., what has been observed or done
- areas of strength are identified as well as points needing development, along with ways whereby the candidate can improve
- action planning involves the candidate's own opinions based on the practical performance and the feedback discussion, e.g., *"As a result of this discussion what do you feel we ought to set as your action points?"*
- negotiation of an action plan still leaves room for the tutor/assessor to insert an item of particular importance as noted from the observation, but which might not be included in the candidate's own contribution. The negotiation comes in agreeing which of the candidate's contributions are rated of less importance than the tutor/assessor's points. Three is probably a maximum number of points for any one action plan
- the action plan is clearly understood by the candidate
- the action plan indicates not only what has to be achieved, but also **details possible methods of achieving it**, e.g., *"Increase your knowledge of physiology"* is not very helpful, whilst, *"Increase your knowledge of physiology by reading pages 123... in book xyz"*, is quite specific and far more useful as an action plan.

Giving the decision or outcome - check that:

- no matter when the decision or outcome is given, one thing is constant - **it should be absolutely clear to the candidate as to where they stand**. If the NGB has aligned its qualifications with NVQs there are only two possibilities to be used in giving the decision - either, *"I believe you to be competent"*, or, *"I believe you to be not yet competent"*. Phrases like, *"You're generally OK, but..."*, or, *"That wasn't bad"*, are avoiding the issue and have not given a candidate a clear understanding of the outcome
- the candidate is treated with dignity. Nobody should be made to feel stupid when receiving a decision on his or her performance. They are people/customers first, candidates second
- the tone of voice and method of providing the decision supports the above. It is not only what is being said, but the method of saying it
- the appropriate paperwork **clearly** indicates the decision/outcome. There should be no misunderstandings
- with few exceptions, the final decision is not really a surprise to the candidate. If the previous assessments have flagged up areas of concern and the candidate has had time to address them, but still fails to be *competent,* then it is unlikely to be surprise. However, to be declared *Not yet competent* in something about which the candidate had received no inkling of weakness should be a very rare occurrence, and which would need serious consideration by the tutor/assessor
- consideration is given to the timing of the decision, e.g., at the beginning, in the middle or at the end of the feedback. Whatever happens the outcome should be linked with action plan detailing how improvements can be implemented.

The Internal Verifier/Moderator

Previously, in paragraph 5.2, *The Assessment Process – What is involved?*, the role of the IV was explained. Tutor/assessors should make every effort to thoroughly understand the role of the Internal Verifier/Moderator so that they can ensure that it is being carried out effectively. Remember, Internal Verifier/Moderator standards and their application are not a one way "happening" or experience. Every one concerned with the assessment process should not only know their own part in it, but should also be aware of the role played by others so that the chances of misunderstandings arising are reduced. The ultimate role of the Internal Verifier/Moderator is that of quality control on behalf of the National Governing Body of the sport and, ultimately, if the NGB is aligned to NVQs, to the Awarding Body, e.g., City and Guilds.

The Internal Verifier/Moderator must be seen as impartial and ensures that candidates have the same decision/outcome no matter who is tutoring/assessing or where it is taking place. The Internal Verifier/Moderator also applies the **National** standards. If differences of opinion occur between Internal Verifier/Moderator and tutor/assessors they should be resolved in private through discussion based on evidence received. The Internal Verifier/Moderator should not be seen as a threat to either candidates or tutors/assessors.

Whilst, technically, the IV may not seem of direct importance to candidates, it is essential that that tutor/assessors fully explain the assessment process, including the roles of both the Internal and External Verifiers.

The IV and practical work

Less experienced tutor/assessors should be aware that there are several ways in which an Internal Verifier/Moderator might approach the task. The two most common are:

- On arrival, the Internal Verifier/Moderator makes social exchanges and then consults the tutor/assessor about any problem candidates. After that s/he observes the candidates concerned, plus a selection of other following the observations the Internal Verifier/Moderator will discuss findings with the tutor/assessor by asking for the tutor/assessor's previous assessment evidence and decisions.
- Arrival as above, but the IV makes own selection of who to sample without reference to the tutor/assessor, observes and then asks for tutor/assessor's evidence on the selected sample of candidates.

Tutor/assessors should remember, it is their role to assess, i.e., make decisions, not the Internal Verifier/Moderator's.

If the IV carries out the role effectively:
- conflicting advice to candidates will be avoided
- the tutor/assessor will be helped in identifying areas which might need addressing
- something the tutor/assessor has said or done may be reinforced
- a topic might be opened up for the tutor/assessor to follow up later.

The logbook/portfolio of evidence

The logbook/portfolio is often one of the three assessment areas in which the candidate must be successful and should be taken very seriously by both candidate and tutor/assessor. The material required for the logbook/portfolio should be marked in detail. Again, the Internal Verifier/Moderator is responsible for sampling on a percentage basis as described earlier. Remember, it is also possible that the External Verifier might also call for samples.

The marking of theory papers

In some NGBs this is the sole responsibility of the IV (100% sample), whilst in others, a different sampling process is carried out. In spite of any difference in method it is useful for tutor/assessors to explain to their candidates how the marking might be carried out and a reference to this will be found in Part 7, paragraph 7.6, *Marking of Theory Work*.

Part 6

Evaluating
and
Reviewing the Course

6.1   Introduction to Evaluations

Any education and training activity needs very careful evaluation both during the actual programme and after its completion. Teachers/coaches are trained to evaluate - good tutoring/assessing also demands the same treatment.

For the purpose of this book the term "evaluation" means the method whereby tutors measure the totality of the course process and delivery, with a view to the evaluation outcomes influencing future courses. It is, therefore, about the end product, rather than the equally important evaluation of the individual sessions.

Teachers/coaches measure the performance of their athletes by reference to a variety of criteria, e.g., achieving a personal best, increasing the length of throw, accuracy of passes, swimming 5 metres unaided for the first time, and so on. Tutors should try to extend the teacher/coach insights into evaluation by getting them to consider their own performance as teacher/coaches, i.e., what have **they** got to do to improve **their** performance? The outcomes of this might mean raising such issues as:
● increasing technical knowledge
● increasing the range of voice use
● consider changes to the teaching/coaching position in relation to the group.

In the early stages of developing the skills of self-evaluation the teacher/coaches often focus on what the participants have to do rather than what "I", the teacher/coach, need to do to improve "me". It is equally important that tutors put themselves through the same process, not only for educational reasons, like improving the learning experience of future candidates but, also, for market economy reasons. There will be others out there, locally, running similar courses, often with full programmes booked months ahead. To compete effectively, therefore, means a constant refining and improving of the "product". Actors are only really remembered for their last performance. The award gained 10 years ago does not count! Tutoring can be classed in the same category, so it essential to get the last one right.

6.2   What is Evaluation About?

As suggested in para 6.1, evaluation is not only the final part of a course, it is ongoing and provides information for inclusion as immediate feedback for programme modification, as well as for use in long term planning and development.

Evaluation can be carried out in a variety of ways, one of which should be to encourage the views of others associated with the programme in question.

Self-evaluation
Notes taken during the running of the course concerning the effectiveness of:
● the delivery of practical and theory sessions
● the design, organisation and planning of the course
● the recruitment of candidates and selection of participants
● the venue (both practical and theory facilities)
● this course compared to previous courses at the same venue and other venues.

Evaluation of course by other interested parties
The issue of a course evaluation sheet towards the end of the programme would provide some formal method of obtaining the views of the "customers". Discussion with both the whole course as a group and with individual candidates is part of the exercise. Seeking the opinions of participants and/or their parents, will also provide comment which could be put to good use on future occasions. If the facilities used were in conjunction with another organisation, e.g., a club or school, then discussion with individuals concerned with that organisation would also be very useful.

Internal Verifiers/Moderator feedback on results obtained
One form of feedback which the tutor/assessor will find helpful will be that of the visitor appointed as part of the assessment process, e.g., the Internal Verifier/Moderator. This is likely to be on the topics of the written tests, and will contain general information about questions answered successfully or not so successfully, e.g., *"The question concerning xxx was well answered by all but one of the candidates"*, or *"The question on competition work was answered badly by all but one of the candidates"*. If all or most candidates get something wrong it probably has some connection with the tutor/assessor's treatment of the topic. If one or, possibly, two candidates go astray with the question is likely be something to do with the candidates concerned, e.g., they simply had not done the revision or failed to seek additional help from the tutor/assessor when a problem arose.

The process of evaluation needs the use of criteria. Some examples of the criteria against which a tutor might measure his/her own performance or programme are:

- the ability to communicate clearly
- the ability to communicate with a variety of people, e.g., participants (children, adults), teachers/coaches, visitors to the programme, e.g., those contributing to the assessment process
- the accuracy of technical knowledge, both in the direct sports subject matter, but, also, other indirect areas, e.g., anatomy and physiology
- the ability to assess teacher/coach performance
- the ability to provide feedback and set action plans where key issues are related to future improvement
- the ability to form working relationships with all concerned
- the ability to encourage the "thinking" teacher/coach, i.e., where opportunities are provided to develop problem-solving techniques.

Of course, the trick is to find ways of measuring one's self against these criteria.

The sorts of questions to be considered might include:

- Have the candidates met the tutor on previous courses and come back for more, even though there are other local opportunities?
- Do the candidate teacher/coaches feel that they can ask questions in public without fear of ridicule?
- Do they feel that they can approach the tutor privately if there is something with which they are having difficulty?
- Do they respond to an action plan because they feel it is accurate and helpful, or, simply, because they feel that they have to - or fail?
- Do they feel that they can disagree with the tutor when they have their own ideas, or is there only one right way (the tutor's!) of doing it, so there is no point in trying to discuss anything?
- Did a high percentage of the candidates achieve a successful result?

The above suggestions are not meant to be an exhaustive commentary on the possibilities. But the "thinking" tutor can begin to consider other areas for exploration. The constraints most frequently quoted concerning evaluation are time and money. The insurance salesperson, when a prospective client counters with, *"I can't afford it"*, replies with, *"Surely, for the sake of your loved ones, you can't afford **not** to!"* So it is with evaluation – *"Surely, for the sake of your future candidates, you can't afford **not** to."*

Task 4 – Evaluation

Evaluate an already completed course and use the information gained as part of the preparation for a future course.

Question	Guidance & Examples
What evidence will be required?	Written - notes, questionnaires Spoken – formal questioning What is the full range to be covered?
Complete own entry	
What questions need to be asked?	Written/Spoken to cover range of aspects of course. Examples of range: facilities, resources; ability of participants; presentation skills; times of sessions etc
Complete own entry	
Who will provide the evidence?	Candidates; leisure centre staff; participants; others involved in the programme
Complete own entry	
How will the evidence be recorded?	Written, video/audio tape, spoken
Complete own entry	
How will the analysis of evidence be recorded?	On forms; summary of Y/N results; summary of a, b, c etc
Complete own entry	
How will the results be used?	To identify own areas for improvement To identify own areas of strength To inform others related to the programme To form basis of discussions/negotiations
Complete own entry	
From the above, what needs: Most attention? (a) (b) etc Least attention? (a) (b) etc	Examples: Meeting objectives Tutoring methods Delivery techniques Facilities Organisation Management Assessment techniques Feedback techniques etc
Complete own entry	

6.3   Approaches to Evaluation

An example of a question that might be asked as part of an evaluation might be:

"How do you rate the tutor presentation in the classroom environment?"

Examples of possible methods of recording the responses to this question:

Method 1   Circle one of the following:

Very good   Good   Satisfactory   poor

Any other comments...
If you provide a low rating please comment more specifically on why this was so.

Method 2   Circle one of the following:

Very helpful   Helpful   Not helpful   Unhelpful

Any other comments...
If you provide a low rating please comment more specifically on why this was so.

Method 3   Circle one of the following:
(A being the highest rating, C being satisfactory and E the lowest rating)

A   B   C   D   E

Any other comments...
If you provide a low rating please comment more specifically on why this was so.

NB   *You do not need to put your name on the evaluation form if you do
       not wish to do so.*

6.4 The Evaluation Outcomes – Their use

Having gathered comment on a variety of aspects of the course, the future use of the information needs to be considered. The analysis of the information is the first point to consider. Since it is unlikely that vast numbers of evaluation sheets are being evaluated all at once, it is likely that some simple approaches can be adopted. This would involve listing the questions posed and than inserting the total responses under each heading against each question. So, using the example question, along with, say, Method 3 the result might be:

"How do you rate the tutor presentation in the classroom environment?"

Total number of candidates = 12

Rating	Response	Percentage		
A	2	16.66%	}	
			}	
B	3	25.00%	}	66.66%
			}	
C*	3	25.00%	}	
D	3	25.00%	}	
			}	33.33%
E	1	8.33%	}	

* C = satisfactory

The 33.33% of candidates who were less than satisfied is significant enough to warrant at least a review of classroom presentation techniques. Hopefully, the candidates who gave lower ratings also gave some clues as to why they did so. This would then form the basis of one aspect of the action plan for tutoring the next teacher/coach education programme.

Clearly, whilst many of the comments will be specifically for tutor action, there may be some which need passing to others. For example, comments on the classroom equipment, the heating/ventilation, refreshment facilities etc, probably would be for the action of the centre where the programme had been based and would need to be passed to the appropriate manager.

6.5   The follow up

It important to consider the range of people to whom a follow up communication should be sent. Yes, the "thank you" notes are important. However, used to their fullest, they can form the basis of a "next time" scenario, much of which could be based on information gleaned from evaluation exercises.

Examples of the lessons learned are likely to range over such items as:
- the venue
- the facilities
- the need for, and nature of, any pre-course information sent to candidates
- the need for a possible induction programme prior to the commencement of the course proper
- the possibility of having candidates send assignments by post for marking and feedback
- the order in which course contents are designed
- the ability levels of the participants
- the presentation methods adopted
- the timing for individual assessments
- the nature of the feedback offered
- the liaison work that may have to be carried out with appropriate people associated with the programme
- the costings of future programmes
- the time of the year in which the programmes run in future
- the time of the day when programmes are run, e.g., the availability of participants of younger age groups
- the shape of the programmes, e.g., weekly, weekends.

These follow-up links are better considered sooner, rather than later, after the completion of the event, rather than wait until the next one in the planning phase. Memories fade, lessons learned are forgotten and the course delivered last time is reproduced as the easy way out. But, surely, something must have been learned from that experience.

Part 7

Further Considerations

7.1 Co-Tutoring

There has been a much greater incidence of examples where more than one qualified tutor is involved in the running of a course. Sometimes a slightly less experienced (but qualified) tutor seeks the support of a more qualified tutor in gaining additional experience without the responsibility of a total programme. In other instances, a couple of experienced tutors pool their strengths to create a very powerful team. This is not only good news for the candidates on the course, but it also enables the tutors concerned to use each other as a means of extending their knowledge base in their less strong areas of skills and knowledge. Whilst candidate teachers/coaches gain a great deal from co-tutoring done well, the responsibility on the tutors concerned to get their act together before embarking on the programme is very great indeed. The prime concern is the quality of the programme delivered to the candidates. They must know exactly where they stand in the process.

Regardless of the reasons for co-tutoring, there are some basic "rules" to consider before entering into such a partnership:
● Compatibility – are the tutors concerned likely to get on with each other?
● Professional integrity – do they have **total** trust in each other's professional ability?

Having made a decision to work together then several other areas need to be worked through:
● Agreeing the total course programme - dates, times.
● Allocation of responsibilities - typing/photocopying of course programmes, organising the practical time sessions etc.
● Allocation of tutoring/lecturing tasks - who leads the sessions on anatomy and physiology, biomechanics etc?
● Assessment process - are each of the tutors going to take the responsibility for the assessment of a number of candidates along with all the marking and tutorial support, or is one going to be responsible for the practical assessment and the other the theory assessments? This has to be given very careful thought. The prime consideration is the impact on the candidates, not the tutors' convenience. Alternatively, there are ploys in between these examples, e.g., that both tutors are available for discussion and support, especially if one tutor is particularly busy with a candidate and is simply not

available. This will mean that the two tutors should frequently consult each about the progress of all the candidates on the programme.

- Attendance - will both tutors be present on every occasion, or will there be a mix of occasions when both are present and when only one is present? It is likely that the presence of both tutors would be necessary on the early sessions of the programme.

- Lead tutoring - the allocation of tutoring/lecturing tasks will mean that both tutors will become lead tutors at various times during the programme. For some tutors the idea of not being "up front" all the time might be a difficult concept to handle. Should this be the case such tutors should carefully review the implications of this type of approach. However, one implication for dealing with lead tutoring is that whoever is not the leader on that occasion must learn to remain silent and not join in the presentation or discussions unless specifically invited to do so by the lead tutor. It would be professional good manners for the lead tutor to invite the other tutor at the end if s/he wished to add anything to what had been said. It would be equally good professional manners to ensure that any additional contribution should be very brief! They must keep reminding themselves that they are doing this together because they have total trust in each other's professional integrity.

- Fees – the implications for costing out co-tutoring programmes raise some important issues. Clearly, to double the tutoring fees charged would probably price the programme out of the market. It might be that the programme is costed on the basis of one tutor, but that the proportion allocated to each is based on the attendance time, plus the appropriate travel expenses, and the occasions where both are present are charged out at 50% of the individual attendance cost. There is no one right way which can be declared the answer to this complex issue, but it is important that it is addressed before the programme commences so that the formula is clearly understood by both concerned. Frequently the relationship between the tutors concerned will allow for this to be dealt with easily.

7.2   Tutoring at Different Levels

Most tutors commence their professional career by leading programmes at the lowest level within their NGB programme. This may well be determined by the NGB and its policy for developing tutors. In addition, most tutors apply common sense and feel that their chances of developing as tutors are best served by starting at such a level – some people describe this as increasing their chances of survival!

- Inexperienced tutors - one of the problems that inexperienced tutors experience is the ability to target the appropriate level of work for the lowest level of teacher/coach education programme. In order to qualify as tutors they will have been working at a much higher level and often forget what it was like to start out from the beginning. It is essential that tutors make constant reference to the NGB syllabus for the level of qualification to remind themselves of the content to be covered. Seeking advice from the NGB and experienced tutors will assist in the arriving at the appropriate level for the candidates. Sometimes, the lowest level is crudely defined as for the average "guy or gal" who walks in off the street and says that they know next to nothing about the teaching/coaching of swimming, soccer, netball etc, but wants to start. Inexperienced tutors should remember these starting points and take them to heart.

- Moving on to higher levels of tutoring – once again, the NGB policy may determine this by controlling when and how tutors begin to tutor at higher levels. The key issue for anyone beginning to embark on work at a higher level is confidence in one's technical knowledge at the new level. By implication, movement into higher levels of tutoring means that the candidates on the programme are not only more knowledgeable, but they are also more experienced and will want to test their experience with that of the tutor. Moving up a level, therefore, has inbuilt hazards for the unwary! Apart from being extremely confident in one's ability to handle the increased demands of technical knowledge and organisational implications, one way of developing working at the new level would be to find out if an experienced tutor would allow the inexperienced tutor to attach to one of his/her programmes. Another way might be to try to run the first programme at the new level with smaller numbers of candidates. This, of course, raises the issue of economics and the financial viability of the programme. In spite of that, however, it should not be totally ruled out as one possible option.

7.3   Mentoring

The notion of mentoring in sport at the teacher/coach level is being developed very successfully (See *A Guide to Mentoring Sports Coaches,* by Bill Galvin (1998), published by the National Coaching Foundation). There is a similar need for providing newly trained tutors with good support in their early tutoring programmes. Some NGBs of sport, e.g., the ASA, build this support, designated as mentoring, into their tutor training programmes in a variety of ways.

Essentially, mentors will be appointed on the strength of their experience and understanding of a newly qualified tutor's problems. Furthermore, their responsibility is solely to guide, advise, discuss and generally support the progress of the newly qualified, with the appropriate professional behaviour towards any other tutors connected with the programme being run. Usually, the mentor carries no moderation or internal verification responsibilities whilst undertaking the mentoring role. Other NGBs may also support their newly qualified tutors in a more informal manner but, nevertheless, recognise that support is needed. Mentoring is undoubtedly a valuable area to develop in some way or another. In some instances inexperienced tutors set up their own mentoring support by approaching more experienced tutors for advice. This is frequently successful, providing the tutor acting as the mentor can actually find the significant amount of time necessary to carry out the role whilst leading his/her own course. However, it is important to emphasise that the role of the mentor is to help the inexperienced develop his or her own styles of delivery, communication, etc, and not simply become a clone of the mentor. Certainly, the mentor should be able to question and challenge the tutor to stimulate him/her into arriving at his/her own conclusions as to the way forward, rather than impose the "right" way. Sometimes, an inappropriate mentor is unable to handle the fact that a newly qualified, inexperienced tutor is actually doing a better job than the mentor could do. This situation might well lead to tension, and far less learning will arise from the experience.

7.4 Postal Work and Distance Learning

In Part 2, paragraph 2.12, *Course Design and the Use of Distance Learning,* and Part 3, paragraph 3.3, *Pre-Course Work/Action Plan,* it was suggested that many tutors employed a system of pre-course tuition. This can be achieved through a form of distance learning. Not only does this help the tutor to prepare the candidates adequately for the course ahead, but it also assists the candidates to begin their learning in a guided manner and be better prepared. It encourages candidates to engage in their own study and reading and adjusting to the workloads before the course first meets. Whilst this technique is probably essential for concentrated courses, it can also be adapted for use in less concentrated programmes. This system employed for pre-course work can also be continued during the course allowing the tutor an increased amount of one to one contact with the candidate.

Before embarking on this approach consider the following points:

- Is the task set within the candidate's capabilities?
- Have the candidates adequate resources to complete the task?
- Is the task clearly laid out to enable the candidate to work alone?
- Does the candidate know the learning outcomes?
- Does the candidate know what is required of them?
- Does the candidate understand the time commitment involved in the programme?
- What support will the candidates require?

Another area which can benefit from postal work is that of session plans generated during the course. As suggested in Part 4, paragraph 4.6, *The Testing of Understanding,* the most common technique for dealing with these is that the tutor collects these at the end of the session in which the plans were used. The tutor marks them and returns them to the candidate during the next session. Whilst this technique is extremely successful, it does not address one very important issue namely, the delayed action for the implementation of any feedback provided by the tutor. For example, session plans completed and collected by the tutor for say, the first session of a programme are marked and returned during second session. Meanwhile, the candidate has prepared plans for the second session. The feedback from the tutor, however, can only be implemented in relation to plans constructed for the third session. By adopting a postal system, with the candidates providing stamped, self-addressed envelopes, the tutor can return the candidates' material much earlier and can influence their approach to the second session plans. The earlier feedback and action planning, therefore, will have more impact.

In Part 3, paragraph 3.6, *Planning the Individual Sessions – The detail,* a passing reference was made to the use of the Internet as a source for data gathering. The use of the Internet and e-mail services in general could greatly enhance the quality of distance learning. Not only does it make information more readily accessible but, also, it could greatly increase the ease and quality of communication between tutor and candidate. Candidates could send assignments, have them marked by the tutor and returned, probably opening up opportunities for a faster turn round of material and more immediate feedback on performance. This could not only work for candidates undertaking distance learning study programmes as an addition to the use of the postal system, but also for the candidates registered on the more common "contact time" programmes involving frequent attendance. Again, the notion of being able to provide more immediate results and feedback should be an attractive prospect and one for which tutors should constantly strive.

7.5   Pre-course

There have been several references in the book, including paragraph 7.4 above, to work or meetings described as *"Pre-Course".* This seems to be the most currently used term to describe either work done by candidates prior to the commencement of the course proper, or a meeting held for the purposes of dealing with, say, a logbook/portfolio. Taken at face value the term probably says it all. However, it might raise queries in the minds of some candidates as to the necessity of either completing work or attending the session – they might argue that since it is *"Pre-Course",* it is not part of the course.

Perhaps other descriptive phrases ought to be considered to give greater emphasis to the importance of both the work and the session, and that both are important, integral parts of the course proper. Possible examples of names might be *Course action plan work, Course logbook/portfolio work, Course induction meeting, Course logbook/portfolio day,* etc. Whatever it is called, candidates should be fully aware that pre-course preparation is an essential ingredient for effective learning to occur.

7.6   Marking of Theory Work

This issue was introduced in Part 5, paragraph 5.3, *The Assessment – How is it done?* In the interests of fairness, the marking process needs to be structured no matter whether the marking is of a course test or an examination paper. However, if the papers are for an examination the process needs to be very structured, indeed. Try to ignore the candidate names on the papers until the final additions of marks are made. Then, using any marking guidance provided by the NGB, mark question 1 on all papers, then question 2 on all papers and so on. NGB guidelines are likely to state that any correct answer must receive credit, even if the answers are in every day English, rather than NGB jargon. It is probably better to mark strongly against the criteria on the first marking, then check on a second marking for any candidates on whom the marker feels s/he has been a little hard during the first marking. In this way the marker is less likely to offer sympathy twice over and, so, seriously distort the results!

7.7   Funding

As a matter of raising tutors' awareness about possible funding, it is simply pointed out that it might be possible to access financial support from a variety of sources so that costs for candidate teacher/coaches might be reduced. There are no guarantees in this matter, but possible ways of reducing fees for candidates might be through:
- local Training and Enterprise Councils (TECs) *
- approaching local Further or Higher Education institutions to find out if they have access to Further Education Funding Council (FEFC) funds *
- registering as a Vocational Trainer with the Inland Revenue. This means that, under certain circumstances, the tutor could offer to give tax relief at standard rate on all or part of the fees being charged out to the candidate. The tutor, as the registered Vocational Trainer, would then claim the tax relief given to the candidate from the Inland Revenue at certain times during the year. This system exists currently, but is likely to come to an end in either April 2000 or 2001. The replacement system, if any, is currently unknown.

* It would appear that both TECs and the FEFC will be disbanded in 2001, and will be replaced by a new body, *The Learning and Skills Council.*

No matter where funding is sought, remember, **there are no guarantees.** Furthermore, the constraints for accessing funding are getting tighter and tighter. But, that is not a reason for not trying - Good luck!

The notion of education and training for one life-long job has long gone. Today's rapidly changing environment needs not only new skills but also flexibility on the part of the individual. It is important that candidates on teacher/coach education programmes are encouraged to take ownership of their own learning to enhance the development of any new skills. The Government is encouraging life-long learning by the introduction of *Learning Accounts* which will give individuals opportunities to opt into a variety of schemes appropriate to their needs and aspirations. Those who wish to develop an interest in leisure and sports in general should be encouraged to explore the opportunities presented by any Government scheme of this nature.

7.8 Code of Ethics

High profile court proceedings featuring unprofessional or unethical behaviour of teachers/coaches towards their participants do nothing for the image of sport in general. Tutors should ensure that they fully explain the code of ethics deemed to be appropriate in the NGB in which they are working. Furthermore, tutors should be role models in terms of their behaviour and relationships with both candidates and participants associated with the teacher/coach education programmes they are leading.

7.9 "Always" and "Never"

"Always" and *"Never"* are often used when an experienced person is offering advice to one who is less experienced. Sometimes, particularly in matters of safety, these words are appropriately explicit in relation to the nature of the situation being addressed. However, on many occasions these two words act as serious constraints to an inexperienced person trying to establish a style of teaching/coaching delivery of their own. They are so over-awed by the advice that they feel that it would be wrong to ignore it, after all, *"Bill Bloggs said it – and he must know!"* Occasionally, during the mentoring process, when a candidate tutor has been asked by the mentor why a particular method had been selected the response has been, *"Because my tutor said that was the **only** way to do it"*. If tutors are to develop their own ideas and strategies it is

essential that they are encouraged to think through the pros and cons of their ideas and make decisions accordingly. Be wary of the use of "Always" and "Never", they represent a very long time! Perhaps teachers/coaches should be encouraged to ask themselves three questions as a simple means of judging the success of their sessions:

- Was it safe?
- Did the participants improve?
- Did the participants enjoy it?

Clearly, there are weaknesses in this kind of judgement since the answers may well reflect the standards of the individual candidates. However, it could open up a debate about an individual candidate's progress and some basic standards against which that progress could be measured.

Part 8

Glossary

AVA – Audio Visual Aids, e.g., pictures, audio/video players, overhead projectors etc.

Accredited assessor – One who has achieved competence as an assessor and has been accredited with Training and Development Units D32 and D33 of the Employment National Training Organisation (ENTO – formerly TDLB and EOSC) (See also tutor).

Approved (Assessment) Centre – Centres, e.g., NGBs, approved by an Awarding Body (See below) to co-ordinate the assessment arrangements for the NVQs which they have been approved to offer.

Awarding Body – An organisation, e.g., City and Guilds, approved by QCA (See below) to award NVQs.

Candidate – The teacher/coach following an education programme or course leading to a NGB qualification.

Competence – An ability to carry out a task or skill effectively, rather than simply have the knowledge of how to do it.

Contact time – The time candidates spend under the formal direction or control of the tutor, i.e., on-course time (See also non-contact time).

EAP - Emergency Action Plan

External Verifier (EV) – one who has been accredited with Training and Development Units D35 of the Employment National Training Organisation (ENTO – formerly TDLB and EOSC) and is appointed by an Awarding Body, e.g., a City and Guilds, to monitor the assessment and internal quality assurance of centres approved to offer NVQs. (See also Part 5, paragraphs 5.2, *The Assessment Process – What is involved?* and 5.3, *The Assessment – How is it done?*)

Facilitator – One who leads and assists others by creating opportunities and situations which will contribute to their understanding of ideas, knowledge and skills.

Internal Verifier (IV) – One who has been accredited with Training and Development Units D34 of the Employment National Training Organisation (ENTO – formerly TDLB and EOSC) and is appointed by an Approved (Assessment) Centre, e.g., a NGB, to ensure consistency and quality of assessment within the centre. (See also Part 5, paragraphs 5.2, *The Assessment Process – What is involved?*, and 5.3, *The Assessment – How is it done?*)

Moderator – Sometimes used by NGBs to describe the person appointed to visit a course as part of the assessment process. May carry out a very similar role to that of an Internal Verifier (See also Part 5, paragraphs 5.2, *The Assessment Process – What is involved?*, and 5.3, *The Assessment – How is it done?*).

NGB - National Governing Body, e.g., Football Association, Amateur Swimming Association.

Non-contact time – The time when candidates are working on their own and not under the direction of the course tutor, e.g., preparation time in the evenings or at home (See also contact time).

NOP – Normal Operating Procedures

Participant – The player, runner, swimmer etc who takes part in the sport or activity.

Plenary (Session) – A meeting where all members of the group are present.

Quality and Curriculum Authority (QCA) – This organisation replaced the National Council for Vocational Qualifications in 1997, and its role is to set a coherent and flexible system of National Vocational Qualifications (NVQs or SNVQs in Scotland).

Tools and Techniques – A collection of simple processes that enable tutors to work in a structured way and, hence, deliver training more efficiently.

Tutor – The one who leads teacher/coach education programmes or courses. A tutor is frequently also an accredited assessor (See also accredited assessor).

Witness categories – (See also witness testimony) witnesses can be classified as follows:

Category 1 -   An occupational expert, as defined by the NGB technical definition, and a D32/D33 assessor

Category 2 -   A D32/D33 assessor without occupational competence

Category 3 -   An occupational expert and familiar with the National Standards*, i.e., not holding D32/D33

Category 4 -   An occupational expert but not familiar with the National Standards*

Category 5 -   A non-expert who is also not familiar with the National Standards*

National Standards in this context means the standards in the context of National Vocational Qualifications (NVQs)

Witness testimony – somebody other than the assessor witnessed the evidence being generated, e.g., was present during the session or confirmed that the work was that of the candidate (See also witness categories).